New York, the City in More Than 500 Memorable Quotations

From More Than 500 Authors
(American and Foreign) and
More Than 500 Reference Sources

by
Vladimir F. Wertsman

The Scarecrow Press, Inc.
Lanham, Md., & London
1997

SCARECROW PRESS, INC.

Published in the United States of America
by Scarecrow Press, Inc.
4720 Boston Way
Lanham, Maryland 20706

4 Pleydell Gardens, Folkestone
Kent CT20 2DN, England

British Cataloguing-in-Publication Information Available

Library of Congress Cataloging-in-Publication Data

New York, the city in more than 500 memorable quotations : from more than 500
    authors (American and foreign) and more than 500 reference sources /
    [collected] by Vladimir F. Wertsman.
        p.   cm.
    Includes index.
    ISBN 0-8108-3088-4 (alk. paper)
    1. Quotations, English.   2. Quotations.   I. Wertsman, Vladimir F.,
    1929– .
    PN6081.N545   1997
    974.7' 1—dc20   95-38622
                                                                                          CIP

ISBN 0-8108-3088-4 (cloth: alk. paper)

♾TM The paper used in this publication meets the minimum requirements of
American National Standard for Information Sciences—Permanence of Paper for
Printed Library Materials, ANSI Z39.48–1984.
Manufactured in the United States of America.

I quote others only in order to better express myself.
　　　　　—Michael Eyquem Montaigne (1533–1592),
　　　　　　　　　　　　　　French essayist

Next to the originator of a good sentence is the first quoter of it.
　　　　　—Ralph Waldo Emerson (1803–1882),
　　　　　　　　American philosopher & essayist

A quotation is a handy thing to have about, saving one from the trouble of thinking for oneself if I may.
　　　　　—A. A. (Alan Alexander) Milne (1882–1956),
　　　　　　　　　　　English poet and dramatist

Contents

Acknowledgments

It is axiomatic that a book of quotations—more than any other book—cannot come into existence without the consultation of hundreds of other books and periodicals. Therefore, I would like first to acknowledge all the authors, compilers, editors, and publishers that produced the titles from which I culled the quotations included in this volume.

Second, I would like to express grateful thanks to the numerous colleagues, friends, and other persons who assisted me as I collected information and researched relevant sources. I list them here arranged by the institution or organization for which they work or from which they have retired in the meantime.

BROOKLINE PUBLIC LIBRARY, MASSACHUSETTS: Robert Sullivan, Reference Librarian

BROOKLYN PUBLIC LIBRARY, NEW YORK: George Wolf, Senior Librarian (retired), and Paul Zaplitny, Supervising Librarian

GALE RESEARCH COMPANY, DETROIT: Judith Galens, Anna Sheets, and Robyn Young, Editors

THE NEW YORK HISTORICAL SOCIETY: Deborah Randorf, Reference Librarian

NEW YORK BOARD OF EDUCATION: Francisca Mendoza, Spanish Teacher, Clara Barton High School

THE NEW YORK PUBLIC LIBRARY:
  Donnell Library Center:
    General Reference: Burt Abelson, Supervising Librarian, Lee Johnson, Supervising Librarian
    World Languages Collection: Bosiljka Stevanovic,

Principal Librarian, and Nelida Kahan and Irina
Kuharets, Senior Librarians
Mid Manhattan Library:
General Reference: Rita E. Bott, Supervising Li-
brarian, and Joseph Paladino, Senior Librarian
Lincoln Center for the Performing Arts:
Dance & Drama Circulation: Dan Cherubin and
Theresa Sanchez, both Librarians
Research Libraries:
General Research: Benjamin Burk, Librarian II,
Sibylle Fraser, Librarian II, Ewa Jankowska, Li-
brarian III, Warren C. Platt, Librarian II, and
Marzena Pasek-Hamilton, Librarian I
Periodicals Division: Nadja Ladjen, Librarian III
Slavonic Division: George Estaffy, Library Technical As-
sistant, Tanya Gizdavich, Librarian
US Local History & Genealogy Division: Marisol Borrero
Saks, Librarian III, Robert D. Scott, Librarian II, and Larry
Gunardsen, Librarian II
POLYTECHNIC ACADEMY OF MINSK, BELARUS: Valentina
Mytko, Professor of History and World Culture
*TECHNOLOGY GENERATION & TRAINING COMPANY,
BETHESDA, MARYLAND:* Susan Vince, President
TIME-WARNER COMPANY, NEW YORK: Lester Annenberg,
Principal Librarian (retired), and Glenn Loflin, Head Cat-
aloging & Circulation Department

Preface

This reference book provides a unique collection of over five hundred quotations about New York City that were written between 1524 and 1996. The quotations come from more than five hundred authors, poets, statesmen, artists, composers, mayors, educators, politicians, actors, sportsmen, musicians, scientists, travelers, and others—men and women of various ethnic backgrounds, including not only American but also British, French, German, Italian, Russian, Spanish, Swedish, and other voices.

Despite New York City's reputation and importance as America's foremost multiethnic metropolis—host to the United Nations and the world's leading cultural, educational, artistic, fashion, culinary, and touristic center—standard American reference books of quotations do not treat New York City adequately. Usually, they include no more than a few dozen quotations about the city and in many cases these are older quotations, some obsolete, redundant, or listing incomplete sources of origin. Two valuable sources of quotations about New York City—*Mirror for Gotham: New York as Seen by Contemporaries from Dutch Days to the Present* (1956) by Bayrd Still and *As I Pass, O Manhattan: An Anthology of Life in New York* (1956) by Esther McCullough—have not been updated and are now over forty years old. Mike Marqusee's *New York: An Illustrated Anthology* (1988) has certainly been a welcome addition but it reflects the opinions of only about one hundred notables from America and Europe. Even the *New York Public Library Book of Twentieth-Century American Quotations,* edited by Stephen Donadio, Joan Smith, and others (1992) included only about four dozen quotations, all easily found in other reference books and some lacking source notes. Finally, William Cole's *New York: A Literary Companion* (1992), with about 250 quotations, is a reprint of an earlier booklet (96 pages); it is useful for quick reference, but does not mention the source for each quotation or even the dates of birth and death for the authors of the quotations.

In light of these considerations, I tried to endow the present volume with the features that were frustratingly absent from other works. All the quotations were culled from primary sources wherever possible and from a wide range of works: biographies and autobiographies (diaries, journals, memoirs), fiction, history, travel, poetry, and song and art books, as well as from various newspapers, journals, and magazines. Mostly English titles were included, but some quotes from foreign titles are included with English translations. Entries are arranged alphabetically by author; each entry is numbered and consists of the name of the author, short biographical data (year of birth and death, profession, and so on), and the full text of the quotation. Following the quotation are the year it was written and the source.

In very few cases, when I could not find the date of birth or death of the author of a quotation, I have indicated this by the abbreviation NDA (no data available). There are also explanatory notes at the end of some quotations regarding the circumstances or the meaning of the quotation.

A subject index enables the reader to find quotations on particular topics (e.g., the Statue of Liberty, the Brooklyn Bridge, etc.). And a chronological index facilitates finding quotations from particular centuries and decades, beginning with 1524 (Europe's first encounter with Native Americans in New York) and culminating with the beginning of 1995, when this volume was completed.

New York City is presented here in all its many facets: there are quotations about the city in general, quotations regarding the five boroughs of the city or specific landmarks (the Empire State Building, Radio City Music Hall), as well as those that focus on the characteristics of New Yorkers or New York architecture.

Both positive and negative impressions of New York are included because New York has always generated controversial opinions from native New Yorkers and visitors alike. Some attribute to New York City only superlatives: "capital of the world"

(Kurt Vonnegut), "Jerusalem of journalism" (Jim Bishop), or "noblest of America's symbols" (James Morris). On the other hand, there are those who bestow upon New York only negatives: "cloaca of all depravities of human nature" (Thomas Jefferson), "sucked orange" (Ralph Waldo Emerson), "harlot among the cities" (Bourke Cockran). Of course, there are also many with indifferent views. The truth is that all opinions (positive, negative, neutral) are essentially right because they express subjectively what each person perceived of New York City at a given moment of time. Therefore, it seems to me that the most appropriate words for New York City were written by Douglas Fairbanks, Jr.: "No one has ever been satisfied with descriptions of New York City, because everyone has his own impression of it. . . . Do we love it or hate it? Probably both!"

In conclusion, I hope that this book of quotations, viewed in the broadest sense as a collective interview with hundreds of people of various generations and as a travelogue of the last five centuries, will prove to be a user-friendly companion to students, teachers, librarians, journalists, authors, diplomats, tourists, immigrants, and other readers interested in New York City. Constructive suggestions are always welcome, and eventually may inspire another edition. You may mail suggestions to the author, in care of Scarecrow Press.

Abbreviations and Symbols

b.	year of birth
d.	year of death
NDA	no date available in library catalogs (card, book, computer)
NY	New York, place of publication of a book
NYC	New York City, quotation refers to New York City
NYPL	New York Public Library
NYS	New York State
NYT	New York Times
WWII	World War II

The Quotations

1. **Charles Adams** (1807–1886), American lawyer and diplomat, son of John Quincy Adams, and grandson of John Adams

   Here was a great city [NYC] of busy people. Yet in this city there seemed little of the character of a fixed population and little of external appearance of happiness. . . . Then the activity of competition glares in every street. . . . Then such an intermixture of fashion and poverty. . . . Adventurers dash in for the spoils and the thousand and one bloodsuckers who are found in the haunts of a corrupt city. I should never be anxious to live in such a city. (1830)

   Source: Charles F. Adams. *Diary* (ed. by Aida di Pace Donald and David Donald). Cambridge, MA: Belknap/Harvard University Press, 1964.

2. **Thomas Adams** (1871–1940), American author, scholar, and specialist in urban development

   Men say New York is a warning rather than an example, and then they proceed to make it an example. Outside America New York is America, and its skyscraper a symbol of America. It is not only the largest city in the world, it is the greatest and most powerful that is not a capital of a nation. (1931)

   Note: New York was America's first capital from 1789 to 1790.
   Source: Thomas Adams. *Regional Plan of New York and Its Environs*. New York: Regional Plan, 1929–1931.

3. **James Agate** (1877–1947), British author and critic

   The astonishing thing [in NYC] is still the skyscrapers. . . .
   From far away and in the near distance they are enormously
   impressive: when one gets right under them they vanish and
   one regains one's normal size. . . . I wonder what it is in the
   New York air that enables me to sit up till all hours in the
   night in an atmosphere which in London would make a horse
   dizzy, but here merely clears the brain. (1937)

   Source: James Agate. *Ego 3: Being Still More of the Biography of
   James Agate.* London: Harrap, 1938.

4. **Margaret Chanler Aldrich** (1870–195?), American poet

   At Ellis Island (poem)
   Ye patient aliens! sifting in
   Where trades a fateful welcome burn,
   Bequest your children what you find—
   A land to which all peoples turn. (1900)

   *Note: Ellis Island, in NYC harbor, served as the entry point for im-
   migrants to USA between 1889 and 1943.*
   Source: Hamilton Fish Armstrong, ed. *The Book of New York's
   Verse.* NY: G. P. Putnam's Sons, 1917.

5. **Nelson Algren** (1909–1981), American author and essayist

   New York is the place of casual acquaintances who become
   your Great-and-Good-Friends in *Time* [magazine]. (1963)

   Source: Nelson Algren. *Who Lost an American?* NY: Macmillan,
   1963.

6. **Steve Allen** (1921–   ), American author and short story
   writer

   Even if you've been there a million times, New York always

comes as something of a shock. The moment I stepped off the jetway into the crowded waiting room, I had a sense of hectic motion and throbbing humanity. . . . I was reminded of the first commandment of New York existence: "To survive here, thou shalt be aggressive." (1990)

Source: Steve Allen. *Murder in Manhattan.* NY: Zebra Books, 1990.

7. **Woody Allen** (1935–), American actor, movie director and producer, born Allen Stewart Konigsberg

I not only was totally in love with Manhattan from the earliest memory, I loved every single movie that was set in New York, every movie that began high above the New York skyline. . . . Every detective story, every romantic comedy, every movie about nightclubs in New York . . . To this day, ninety-nine percent of movies that are not in New York City . . . I rarely catch on to. . . . (1991)

Source: Eric Lax. *Woody Allen: A Biography.* NY: Alfred Knopf, 1991.

8. **Jervis Anderson** (1936–), African American author

If Black Harlem was once a heaven, or was seen to be one by the migrants and the commentators of the nineteen-twenties, it has ceased to be that by the beginning of the nineteen-fifties when the early optimism had been exhausted. There remained, among the majority of population, almost all the racial and social hardships that many had hoped would be nonexistent in the finest urban community that blacks had ever occupied in the United States.

Source: Jervis Anderson. *This Was Harlem: A Cultural Portrait, 1900–1950.* NY: Noonday Press/Farrar, Straus & Giroux, 1982.

9. **Sherwood Anderson** (1876–1941) American author and publisher

   I think you know that when an American stays away from New York too long, something happens to him. Perhaps he becomes a little provincial, a little dead, a little afraid. (1940)

   Source: Mike Marqusee and Bill Harris. *New York: An Illustrated Anthology.* Topsfield, MA: Salem House, 1988.

10. **William Archer** (1856–1924), Scottish critic and dramatist

    This is the first sensation of life in New York—you feel that the Americans have practically added a new dimension to space. They move almost as much on the perpendicular as on the horizontal plane. When they find themselves a little crowded, they simply tip a street on end and call it a sky-scraper. (1900)

    Source: William Archer. *America Today: Observations and Reflections.* NY: C. Scribner's Sons, 1900.

11. **Hamilton "Fish" Armstrong** (1893–1973), American journalist

    The Tweed Ring (poem)
    The Great Moguls of Gotham! Their proud purses
    Grow with the rich man's spoil and poor man's curses;
    With a firm grasp on every pocket, they
    Build fanes for which the service people pay.
    The rich and poor they plunder as they will—
    The more the people howl the more they steal; (1868)

    Note: This poem was written by an anonymous poet, but included in the volume edited by this author. Reference is made to William Tweed (1823–1878) and his companions who controlled NYC government and robbed taxpayers of their money.

Source: Hamilton Fish Armstrong, ed. *The Book of New York's Verse*. NY: G. P. Putnam's Sons, 1917.

12. **Harry Ashmore** (1916–), American historian and author

New York is not simply an uncomfortable place to live and work in, but a state of mind, and in that sense there is nothing left now to confine it, no physical barriers and no permanent distinctive regional attitudes. So I was at peace with New York not because I had conquered it, or tried to, but because I had surrendered. (1958)

Note: A newcomer to New York—from the South—explains how he adjusted to the city.
Source: Harry S. Ashmore. *An Epitaph for Dixie*. NY: Norton, 1958.

13. **Isaac Asimov** (1920–1992), American science fiction author

I am certain that nowhere in the world is there so large, so dense, and so continuous a collection of exciting things happening as on the Island of Manhattan, and that nowhere are there so few restrictions on one's choice of life-style. I may leave Manhattan briefly, from time to time, but never voluntarily. (1985)

Source: Roxie Munro. *Color New York*. NY: Timbre/Arbor House, 1985.

14. **Brooke Astor** (1902–), American philanthropist, socialite, editor, trustee of many organizations

The best is all the wonderful things you can see or do [in NYC]. There's anything you could want. The worst is the traffic, all the delays in getting to the wonderful things. (1993)

Source: *New York* (magazine). December 20–27, 1993.

15. **Brooks Atkinson** (1894–1984), American author, biographer

If 1,668,172 people . . . are to be set down in one narrow strip of land [Manhattan] between two quiet rivers, you can hardly improve on this solid mass of buildings and the teeming organism of human life that streams through them. For better or for worse, this is real. . . . All the beauties of Manhattan are manmade. (1964)

Source: *New York Times.* March 17, 1964.

16. **Anthony Bailey** (1933–), American author, fiction and biographies

As one comes down the Henry Hudson Parkway along the river in the dusk, New York is never real, it is always fabulous. (1967)

Source: *The New Yorker,* July 29, 1967.

17. **Ross K. Baker** (1938–), American author

The $100-plus dinner in New York is a major speculative undertaking akin to going after a sunken treasure. . . . The cost of the expedition is going to be steep [and] you'll come out of it enriched or just soaked. (1986)

Source: *New York Times.* October 29, 1986.

18. **Russell Baker** (1925–), American journalist and author

What the New Yorker calls home would seem like a couple of closets to most Americans, yet he manages not only to live there but also to grow trees and cockroaches right on the premises. (1978)

Source: *New York Times.* November 18, 1978.

19. **George Balanchine** (1904–1983), Georgian-American choreographer and ballet master

In New York, nature is considered something completely separated from everyday existence, and so every violent invasion of nature in your life is discussed as a major event ad nauseam. A person ignores nature, so nature finally draws attention to itself and, like every performer ignored for too long, proceeds to chew the scenery. (1982)

Note: Reference is made to storms, blizzards, and so on in New York life.
Source: *New York Times,* January 10, 1996, op-ed page.

20. **James Baldwin** (1924–1987), African American author

All of Harlem is pervaded by a sense of congestion, rather like the insistent, maddening, claustrophobic pounding in the skull that comes from trying to breathe in a very small room with all the windows shut. (1955)

Source: James Baldwin. *Notes of a Native Son.* Boston: Beacon Press, 1955.

21. **Willis T. Ballard** (1903–   ), American author

You can take a boy out of Brooklyn, but you can never get Brooklyn out of the boy. (1942)

Note: Reference is made to Brooklyn customs and especially the specific accent of that borough.
Source: Willis Todhunter Ballard. *Say Yes to Murder.* NY: Mystery House, 1942.

22. **Amiri Baraka** (1934–   ), African American poet, author, and dramatist, born Leroi Jones

I was a stranger in New York. I had no phone, I couldn't

even call anybody. That's a lonely feeling. But I had an apartment and a job. I was in New York on my own, by my lonesome, and that was good enough for me. (1960s)

Note: Refers to author's life in Greenwich Village after moving from New Jersey.
Source: Amiri Baraka. *Autobiography of Leroi Jones.* NY: Freundlich Book, 1984.

23. ***Barnard College Bulletin*** (1901–   ), Weekly publication of Barnard College-Columbia University, NYC

All its [NYC] inhabitants ascend to heaven right after their death, having served their full term in hell right on Manhattan Island. (1967)

Source: Editorial of September 22, 1967

24. **Djuna Barnes** (1892–1982), American author, poet, and columnist

New York is a meeting place of the peoples, the only city you can hardly find a typical American. (1916)

Source: Djuna Barnes. *Djuna Barnes's New York.* Los Angeles: Sun and Moon Press, 1989.

25. **James Barron** (1944–   ), American author and journalist

Clearly, it was not just another night in the most literary of cities. Best-selling authors juggled pots and pans in the kitchen. Bleary-eyed manuscript readers mingled with tycoons whose main daily reading matter is stock tables. And from private midtown clubs to minimalist SoHo lofts to Upper East Side town houses, they all toasted a singularly New York institution, the New York Public Library.

Note: New York Public Library's 100th Anniversary was cele-

brated on December 6, 1995, at 100 private dinner parties.
(1995)
Source: *New York Times,* December 7, 1995

26. **Jack Barry** (1918–1984), American entertainer, television game show host

    The trouble with New York is it's so convenient to everything I can't afford. (1952)

    Source: *Reader's Digest.* December 1952.

27. **Maurice Barrymore** (1847–1905), English actor and author, father of famous Lionel Barrymore

    This is Broadway, the longest street with the shortest memory. (1890s)

    Source: Herbert V. Prochnow, ed. *Speaker's Epigrams and Witticisms.* NY: Harper & Row, 1955.

28. **Roland Barthes** (1915–1980), French author and semiologist

    New York . . . is a city of geometric heights, a petrified desert of grid and lattices, an inferno of greenish abstraction under a flat sky, a real Metropolis from which man is absent by his very accumulation. (1959)

    Source: Roland Barthes. *The Eiffel Tower and Other Mythologies* (transl. from the French by Richard Howard). NY: Hill and Wang, 1979.

29. **Jacques Barzun** (1907–   ), American author, music and literary critic, teacher

    New York is the Mecca of everyone in the world who has an

independent will and conception of the century he lives in. New York is the gateway to the 48 states' freedoms—which may not be enough, but which are unquestionably better than the seven devils left behind. New York means all this and earns its greatness, but by a paradox of equal magnitude, it fails in all the practical modernity it supposedly stands for. (1954)

Note: The seven devils Barzun refers to are the seven deadly sins. In the Middle Ages, the seven deadly sins were attributed to art and literature.
Source: Jacques Barzun. *God's Country and Mine: A Declaration of Love Spiced with Harsh Words.* NY: Vintage Books, 1954.

30. **Jean Baudrillard** (1929–   ), French author and semiologist

Cities are . . . distinguished by the catastrophic forms they presuppose and which are a vital part of their essential charm. New York is King Kong, or the blackout, or vertical bombardment: towering inferno. Los Angeles is horizontal fault. . . . (1983)

Source: Jean Baudrillard. *Fatal Strategies.* London: Semiotexte Plato, 1983.

◆ ◆ ◆

It [NYC] is a world completely rotten with wealth, power, senility, indifference, puritanism and mental hygiene, poverty and waste, technological futility and aimless violence, and yet I cannot help but feel it has about it something of the dawning in the universe. (1986)

Source: Jean Baudrillard. *America* (transl. from the French by Chris Turner). New York: Verso Publishers, 1988.

31. **Jessie Tarbox Beals** (1870–1942), first American woman news photographer

I miss New York and its fairy-like towers
With Liberty's torch high in the air
I'd give all of California's damn flowers
For the sight of Washington Square. (1936)

Source: Alexander Alland. *Jessie Tarbox Beals: First Woman News Photographer.* NY: Camera Graphic Press, 1978.

32. **Cecil Beaton** (1904–1980), English designer and photographer

New York appears to be a great city in a great hurry. The average street pace must surely be forty miles an hour. The traffic lights switch straight from red to green without any nonsense about orange symbolizing the harshness of contrast that dispenses with the intermediate things that Europeans respect. It is usually unwise to cross the road except in accordance with the green light, and even New York dogs are said to understand this symbol. (1938)

Source: Cecil Beaton. *Portrait of New York.* London/NY: B.T. Batsford, 1948.

33. **Simone de Beauvoir** (1908–1986), French author and essayist

There is something in New York air that makes sleep useless. . . . Never had misery appeared so horrible as in New York and Chicago. (1953)

Source: Simone de Beauvoir. *America Day by Day* (transl. from the French by Patrick Dudley). NY: Grove Press, 1953.

34. **Brendan Behan** (1923–1964), Irish author, poet, and artist

I am not afraid to admit that New York is the greatest city on the face of God's earth. . . . New York is easily recognizable as the greatest city in the world, view it any way and every way—back, belly, all sides. (1964)

Source: *New York Post.* March 22, 1964.

◆ ◆ ◆

New York is my Lourdes, where I go for spiritual refreshment. . . . A place where you're least likely to be bitten by a wild goat. (1964)

Source: Brendan Behan. *Brendan Behan's New York.* NY: Bernard Geis Associates, 1964.

35. **Alan Behr** (NDA), American journalist

New York at Christmas is about shopping and giving, about office parties and holiday bonuses, about answered pleas to assist the poor, about family gatherings in under-sized apartments. At Christmas in this, the world's most prosaic financial capital, life can almost reach the level of poetry. (1994)

Source: *Boston Sunday Globe.* October 2, 1994 (article by Alan Behr).

36. **Saul Bellow** (1915–   ), American author, Nobel Prize winner for literature (1976)

I think that New York is not the cultural center of America, but the business and administrative center of American culture. (1969)

Source: *Listener* (British publication). May 22, 1969.

◆ ◆ ◆

New York makes one think of the collapse of civilization, about Sodom and Gomorrah, the end of the world. The end wouldn't come as a surprise here. Many people already bank on it. (1970)

Source: Saul Bellow. *Mr. Sammler's Planet* (part IV). NY: Viking Press, 1970.

37. **Ludwig Bemelmans** (1898–1962), American painter, illustrator, and author

I regard it [Manhattan] as a curiosity: I don't let myself get caught in the wheels. (1951)

Source: *Time* (magazine). July 2, 1951.

38. **Robert Benchley** (1889–1945), American author, humorist

For most visitors to Manhattan, both foreign and domestic, New York is the Shrine of the Good Time. This is only natural, for outsiders come to New York for the sole purpose of having a good time, and it is for their New York hosts to provide it. (1940s)

Source: Babette Rosmond. *Robert Benchley: His Life and Good Times*. Garden City, NY: Doubleday, 1970.

39. **Thomas Bender** (1934–   ), American author on education topics

The City of New York has been the historic point of entry not only for European immigrants but also for European ideals and cultural ideas. Neither European immigrants nor European ideals have made New York over in their own image, but neither were they simply assimilated into a fixed native society. What is interesting in both cases is the play of experiences and cultures. (1987)

Source: Thomas Bender. *New York Intellect: A History of Intellectual Life in New York City from 1750 to the Beginnings of Our Time*. NY: Alfred Knopf, 1987.

40. **Meyer Berger** (1891–1957), American journalist, NYT columnist

People who come from less crowded cities are shocked when they find themselves in the race [in NYC]. . . . Men and women have written bitterly about it; have applied the literary quirt to New York and to its people. Some of it is justified, but mainly it comes from hasty judgement. Back in their homes, city dwellers are normal folks, content with normal living. They follow humble, normal family routines. (1959)

Source: Meyer Berger. *Meyer Berger's New York.* NY: Random House, 1960.

41. **Laurence Bergreen** (1956–), American author and biographer

In its size and delicacy it [the Chrysler Building] resembled a Latter-Day Chartres built in praise of a new God, the holy dollar. . . . In the lobby, the latest model Chrysler revolved on a pedestal, as if the automobile were an object of reverence. (1984)

Source: Laurence Bergreen. *James Agee: A Life.* NY: Dutton, 1984.

42. **Claire Berman** (1936–), American author and journalist

In no other city or suburb are youngsters offered so much for their entertainment, education, recreation and stimulation than in New York. . . . Not only is New York a great city for kids, it is also a great city for the adults who are bringing up their children here, for seeing New York through a child's eyes is to see everything anew. (1969)

Source: Claire Berman. *A Great City for Kids: Parent's Guide to a Child's New York.* NY: Bobbs-Merrill, 1969.

43. **Sarah Bernhardt** (1844–1923), French actress and author, born Henriette-Rosine Bernard

It [the Brooklyn Bridge] is insane, admirable, imposing, and it makes one feel proud to be a human being when one realizes that a human brain has created and suspended in the air fifty yards from the ground, that fearful thing which bears a dozen trains filled with passengers, ten or twelve tramcars, a hundred cabs, and thousands of passengers, and all that moving together amidst the uproar of the music of the metals. (1906)

Source: Sarah Bernhardt. *Memories of My Life*. NY: Benjamin Bloom, 1968 (reprint of 1908 ed.).

44. **Jacob Bigelow** (1786–1879), American physician and educator

Emporium Versus New York (poem)
With head erect and stately pride,
In Broadway, on the Western Side,
I marched, and viewed in conscious pride,
The splendors of New York. . . . (1854)

Source: Hamilton Fish Armstrong, ed. *The Book of New York's Verse*. New York: G. P. Putnam's Sons, 1917.

45. **Isabella Bird** (1832–1904), British author and traveler

Strangers frequently doubt whether New York possesses a police; the doubt is very justifiable . . . for the guardians of the public peace are seldom forthcoming when they are wanted. They are accessible to bribes, and will investigate into a crime when liberally rewarded, but probably in no city in the civilized world is life so fearfully insecure. The practice of carrying concealed arms, in the shape of stilettoes for attack, and sword-sticks for defence, if illegal, is perfectly common. . . . (1854)

Source: Isabella Bird. *The English Woman in America*. London: John Murray, W. Clowells, 1854.

46. **Stephen Birmingham** (1932–), American author

New York remains a city—like London, Paris, Rome and Madrid—where the wealthy still find it pleasant to spend the majority of their time, and where the not so wealthy still have faith in the tantalizing possibilities of success. . . . New York is still a city where success is the main industry—a one company town in a sense, a city of aspiration. (1979)

Source: Stephen Birmingham. *Life at the Dakota: New York's Most Unusual Address*. NY: Random House, 1979.

47. **James Blake** (1862–1935), American lyricist

The Sidewalks of New York (song)
East Side, West Side, all around the town,
The tots sang "Ring-a-rosie", "London Bridge is falling down"
Boys and girls together, me and Mamie O'Rourke,
Tripped the light fantastic on the sidewalks of New York . . .
(1898)

Note: Music by Charles B. Lawlor (1914–)
Source: *Fake Book of the World's Favorite Songs*. Winona, MN: Hall Leonard Publishing, 1990.

48. **Ken Bloom** (1952–), American author, music topics

Times Square is the only spot where the hundreds of different worlds that comprise New York City meet face to face. The result has been funny, dramatic and sometimes deadly. Times Square mixes hookers, Broadway stars, gangsters, newspapermen, schnorrers, and bon vivants, rubber neckers and passersby. These worlds all coexist in 10 blocks of Broadway. (1991)

Source: Ken Bloom. *Broadway: An Encyclopedic Guide to the History, People and Places of Times Square*. NY: Facts on File, 1991.

49. **Judy Blume** (1936–   ), American author of juvenile literature

No place has delicatessen like New York [City]. (1970)

Source: Judy Blume. *Are You There God? It's Me Margaret*. Scarsdale, NY: Bradbury Press, 1970.

50. **James Boardman** (NDA), British businessman and traveler

My first impressions, on landing in New York—and they were subsequently confirmed—were the high character and appearance of the working classes . . . The carters, workmen, and others, who earn their bread by the sweat of their brow, appeared extremely well clothed, were intelligent, and if addressed civilly, were civil in return, yet . . . without the slightest approaches of servility (1833)

Note: *Boardman describes New York during his trip in 1829–1831.*
Source: James Boardman. *America and the Americans . . . By a Citizen of the World*. London: Longman, Rees, Orme, Brown, 1833.

51. **Cesare Bonnano** (1889–   ), American, NYC oldest retired detective, walked beat in 1915

There was always a guy in the station house [in NYC] on the shady side. . . . You'll never wipe it out—you'll never stop it. (1994)

Note: *Comment regarding corruption in NYC police ranks and the fight against it.*
Source: *New York Post*. August 1, 1994.

52. **Jorge Luis Borges** (1899–1986), Argentinian author and scholar

    A good place to dream . . . I love Buenos Aires, where I live, and London and Paris, but New York is like ancient Rome, the capital of the world. (1967)

    Note: Remark was made during a visit in 1967.
    Source: Alfred Kazin. *Our New York*. NY: Harper & Row, 1989 (introduction).

53. **Dion Boucicault** (1820–1890), Irish actor and dramatist, also known as Bourcicault

    It [NYC] was not a city. It was a theatre. It was a huge fair. Bunting of all nationalities and of no nationality was flaunting over the streets. Poles of liberty accentuated the "Rights of Man." . . . Irish was spoken in the wharves, German in the saloons, French in the restaurants. But the chiefest feature in this polyglot city was its boyhood. A boy in heart, but a man, and a very shrewd one, in head. (1889)

    Source: *North American Review*. August 1889.

54. **Paul Bourget** (1852–1935), French novelist, poet, and critic

    This [NYC] is a table of contents of unique character, arranged for convenient handling. Seen from here it is so colossal, it encloses so formidable an accumulation of human efforts, as to overpass the bounds of imagination. You think you must be dreaming when you see beyond the rivers two other cities—Jersey City and Brooklyn—spread but along their shores. (1893)

    Source: Paul Bourget. *Outre-Mer: Impressions of America*. NY: C. Scribner, 1895.

55. **William (Bill) Bradley** (1943–   ), American basketball player and politician, U.S. Senator

I like the rough impersonality of New York, where human relations are oiled by jokes, complaints, and confessions— all made with the assumption of never seeing the other person again. I like New York because there are enough competing units to make it still seem a very mobile society . . . because it engenders high expectations simply by its pace. (1976)

Source: Bill Bradley. *Life on the Run*. NY: Quadrangle/New York Times Books, 1976.

56. **William J. Bratton** (1947–   ), NYC Police Commissioner

We are going to over the next several years, spend a lot of time and a lot of money . . . on identifying why is it that so many New York cops treat people in a disrespectful way, we are going to have major campaigns under way to deal with this issue. . . . As crime goes down, people's fear goes down. All of that is going to be of no avail if the public . . . is not treated in a respectful way, which is the case too frequently. (1994)

Source: *New York Times*. November 28, 1994.

57. **Jimmy Breslin** (1940–   ), American author

People born in Queens, raised to say each morning they get on the subway and "go to the city" have a resentment of Manhattan, of the swiftness of its life and success of the people which live there. (1986)

Source: Jimmy Breslin. *Table Money*. NY: Ticknor & Fields, 1986.

58. **Alan Brien** (1925–   ), American author

New York waiters, probably the surliest in the Western World, . . . are better images of their city than the journalistic favorite—the taxi driver. (1966)

Source: *Saturday Review*. February 5, 1966.

59. **Iosif Brodsky** (1940–   ), Russian American poet, Nobel Prize winner for literature (1987)

In Europe proportions are different. There, the buildings even if they are very tall, nevertheless they are under the control of your imagination. However, in New York, both the building proportions and imagination are completely set aside, they do not have any relationship with reality. (1990)

Source: Marianna Volkova and Solomon Volkov. *Brodskii in New York: Pictures & Interviews*. NY: Slovo, 1990 (title and quotation translated from the Russian text).

60. **Sir Denis Brogan** (1900–1974), British historian

One of the few charms that Manhattan has for me is its nearly complete freedom from one of the most annoying of American habits: impertinent curiosity about other people's affairs. (1964)

Source: *Encounter* (British publication). June 1964.

61. **Rupert Brooke** (1887–1915), English poet and playwright

It is fine—until you get near enough to see its clumsiness. A hand fell on my shoulder, and a voice said "Look hard at that, young man! That's the first time you've seen Liberty—and it will be the last until you turn back on this country again. (1916)

Note: Author's feelings about the Statue of Liberty.

Source: Rupert Brooke. *Letters from America*. NY: C. Scribner's Sons, 1916.

62. **Eve Brown** (1901–   ), American author, pseudonym of Mary Eudora Nichols

For three generations of New Yorkers, the majestic Plaza [Hotel] . . . offered reassurance that a way of life would survive wars, depressions, even death. She was elegant, yet sturdy, bulwark against all that was brash and mediocre, removed in spirit from the frenzied modern pace, indifferent to encroaching high-rise steel and chrome, serenely secure in her fine heritage. . . . Nothing could disturb her well-ordered existence. (1967)

Source: Eve Brown. *The Plaza: Its Life and Times*. NY: Meredith Press, 1967.

63. **Henry C. Brown** (1862–1961), American author and historian

All the world came to Broadway, to shop, to dine, to flirt, to find amusement, and to meet acquaintances. . . . Pen and pencil of the writer and draughtsman always found contrasting types of interest on Broadway. And the weeklies gave a little series of portraits by a notable delineator in both arts of the town's celebrities. (1898)

Source: Henry Brown. *In the Golden Nineties*. Hastings-on-Hudson, NY: Valentine Manuals, 1928.

64. **Katherine Brush** (1902–1952), American author

New Yorkers are nice about giving you street directions; in fact they seem quite proud of knowing where they are themselves. (1940s)

Source: A. K. Adams. *Home Book of Humorous Quotations*. NY:
Dodd, Mead & Co., 1969.

65. **Pearl Buck** (1892–1973), American novelist and short story
writer

As for New York City, it is a place apart. There is not its
match in any other country in the world. (1971)

Source: Pearl Buck. *Pearl Buck's America*. NY: Bartholomew
House, 1971.

66. **Sue Burchard** (1937–   ), American librarian, and author of
books for young readers

As she approaches her hundredth birthday, she is being well
taken care of and is cherished not only by Americans but also
by people everywhere as a symbol of liberty and freedom. It
is said that the centennial restoration will enable the Statue
of Liberty to withstand conditions in New York harbor for
the next thousand years. That's a pretty impressive predic-
tion, but most of us would like to think she will be there forever. (1969)

Source: Sue Burchard. *The Statue of Liberty*. NY: The New York
Times Company, 1969.

67. **Kenneth Burke** (1897–NDA), American poet, drama and
literary critic

. . . New York and not Paris is the true cosmopolis, because
in New York they have to speak different languages,
whereas in Paris languages other than French are spoken
simply as a sort of high-grade snobbism; but that makes
Paris the intellectual cosmopolis. . . . (1917)

Source: Kenneth Burke. *The Selected Correspondence of Kenneth*

Burke and Malcolm Cowley, 1915–1981 (ed. by Paul Jay). NY: Viking Press, 1988.

68. **Witter Bynner** (1881–1961), American poet, critic, editor

We sped to New York. . . . I barely saw my brother who lives there but who is himself so saturated with New York. . . . New York is not a pleasant place . . . and I suppose New York would have been good too, if I had learned the wisdom of focusing, instead of stepping into the kaleidoscopic vertigo. (1948)

Source: Witter Bynner. *The Works of Witter Bynner: Selected Letters* (ed. by James Kraft). NY: Farrar, Straus, 1981.

69. **Herbert Caen** (1916–   ), American author

When can a city be said to be dying? For one thing, when its past far outshines its present and overwhelms the future, and New York is at that point. The giants have gone, along with the good days and easy nights. (1976)

Source: Herbert Caen. *One Man's San Francisco*. Garden City, NY: Doubleday, 1976.

70. **Erskine Caldwell** (1903–1987), American author

Young writers should never let themselves be lured to New York to live and try to write. . . . Young writers should live among their own people so their roots can thrive and take nourishment from their heritage. . . . Promising young writers come to New York and lose their direction. (1930s)

Note: Author's recollection of advice given by a literary agent at the beginning of the author's career.
Source: Erskine Caldwell. *With All My Might (An Autobiography)*. Atlanta, GA: Peachtree Limited, 1987.

71. **John Cale** (1940–   ), British rock musician

I like it here in New York. I like the idea of having to keep eyes in the back of your head all the time. (1989)

Source: *Times* (London). September 27, 1989.

72. **Alexander Callow Jr.** (1925–   ), American historian and author

For five years the Tweed Ring has led a great treasury raid. . . . Tammany Hall had been remodeled into an awesome political machine, supported by the immigrant and the native poor, and sustained on the election day by a horde of Tammany warriors, repeaters, and corrupt election officials who made a mockery out of the power of the ballots. (1871)

Note: Reference is made to William Tweed (1823–78). See entry 11.
Source: Alexander B. Callow Jr. *The Tweed Ring.* NY: Oxford University Press, 1966.

73. **James Cameron** (1911–   ), British author

I love short trips to New York; to me it is the finest three-day town on earth. (1966)

Source: James Cameron. *Witness.* London: V. Gollancz, 1966.

74. **Albert Camus** (1913–1960), French (Algerian born) philosopher, author, and dramatist, Nobel Prize winner for Literature (1957)

This orgy of violent lights [in Manhattan] gives for the first time the impression of a new continent. An enormous 50-foot high Camel billboard: A GI with his mouth wide open blows enormous puffs of real smoke. So much bad taste hardly seems imaginable. (1946)

Source: Albert Camus. *American Journals* (transl. from the French by Hugh Levick). NY: Paragon Press, 1987.

75. **Truman Capote** (1924–1984), American author

It [Brooklyn Heights] stands atop a cliff that secures a sea-gull's view of Manhattan and Brooklyn bridges, of lower Manhattan's tall dazzle and the ship-lane waters, breeding river to bay and ocean, that encircle and seethe past posturing Miss Liberty. . . . Of . . . seeming mirages, the purest example is the neighborhood in which I am situated, an area known as Brooklyn Heights. (1957)

Source: Andrea Wyatt Sexton and Alice Leccese Powers, eds. *The Brooklyn Reader: 30 Writers Celebrate America's Favorite Borough.* New York: Harmony Books, 1994.

76. **Margaret Carthy** (1911–1992), American author, Catholic leader

Never in the lifetime of anyone now walking the streets of the city [NYC] has St. Patrick's Cathedral looked so beautiful. It is immaculate within and without, and the copper figure of the Virgin Mary . . . above the roof of the Lady chapel is a sign of affection. . . . She smiles down upon us as we hurry past along Madison Avenue. (1984)

Source: Margaret Carthy. *A Cathedral of Suitable Magnificence: St. Patrick's Cathedral New York.* Wilmington, DE: Michael Glazier, 1984.

77. **Louis-Fernand Céline** (1894–1961), French author and playwright, born Louis Destouches

In Africa I had indeed found a sufficiently frightful kind of loneliness but the isolation of this American ant heap [NYC] was even more shattering. (1932)

Source: Louis-Fernand Céline. *Journey to the End of the Night* (transl. from the French). NY: New Directions, 1980.

78. **Michel de Certeau** (1925–1986), French author and critic

New York has never learned the art of growing old by playing on all its pasts. Its present invents itself, from hour to hour, in the act of throwing away its previous accomplishments and challenging the future. A city composed of paroxysmal places in monumental reliefs. (1974)

Source: Michel de Certeau. *The Practice of Everyday Life* (transl. from the French by Steven Rendall). Berkeley, CA: University of California Press, 1984.

79. **Fyodor Chaliapin** (1873–1938), Russian opera singer, performed basso roles

The statue personifying Liberty has been exiled out of town and stands outside the gates; it is evidently offended. . . . [I]n my opinion, her eyes look towards Europe, and she must think that in that faraway place there is some slight hope and that if only she could, she would cross the waves of the ocean to come to us in Europe. (1908)

Source: Victor Borovsky. *Chaliapin: A Critical Biography*. NY: Alfred Knopf, 1988.

80. **John Jay Chapman** (1862–1933), American essayist and memorialist

The present in New York is so powerful that the past is lost. (1909)

Source: John Jay Chapman. *John Jay Chapman and His Letters* (ed. by M. A. de Wolfe Howe). Boston: Houghton Mifflin, 1937.

81. **Charles II** (1630–1685), King of England

You will have heard of our taking of New Amsterdam . . . It did belong to England before, but the Dutch by degrees drove our people out and built a very good town, but we have got the better of it, and 'tis now called New York. (1664)

> *Note: Quotation from a letter written by Charles II on October 24, 1664, one of the earliest documents mentioning the name of New York.*
> Source: *Who Said What When: A Chronological Dictionary of Quotations.* London: Bloomsbury Publishing, 1988.

82. **Jerome Charyn** (1937–   ), American, Bronx (NYC)-born fiction author

I grew up in . . . a ghetto called Morrisania, which had its own Black Belt on Boston Road, and a strip of bodegas under the trucks of Southern Boulevard, a wall of Irish surrounding Crotona Park, and a heartland of Italians and Jews, poor as hell, except for a handful of furriers, accountants, lonely physicists, and our congressman, who lived on Crotona Park East. (1940s)

> *Note: Morrisania is a neighborhood in the borough of Bronx, NYC*
> Source: Jerome Charyn. *Metropolis: New York as Myth, Market Place and Magical Land.* NY: G. P. Putnam's Sons, 1986.

83. **W. Parker Chase** (NDA), American author and historian

NEW YORK—Mecca which lures the brightest minds, the most brilliant writers, the most masterful artisans to its gates! NEW YORK—home of the world's greatest captains of industry, the world's most stupendous structures, the world's richest business institutions—veritable center of our country's wealth, culture and achievement! NEW YORK—

!!! What visions of magnitude, variety and power the name NEW YORK conjures up for human comprehension. (1931)

Source: W. Parker Chase. *New York, The Wonder*. NY: Wonder City Publishing, 1931.

84. **George Chauncey** (1927–), American author, writes on gay topics

New York was full of single men and women who had left their families in southern Europe or the American South or whose work on the seas made New York one of their many temporary home ports. Countless men had moved to New York in order to participate in the relatively open gay life available there, and the waterfront, the Bowery, Times Square and other centers of transient workers had become a major center of gay life. (1994)

Note: Chauncey describes New York during 1900–1940.
Source: George Chauncey. *Gay New York: Gender, Urban Culture and the Making of the Gay Male World, 1890–1940*. NY: Basic Books, 1994.

85. **John Cheever** (1912–), American author and storyteller

I don't suppose there was a day, an hour, when the middle class got their marching orders, but toward the end of the 1940s the middle class began to move. . . . [T]he rich of the city [NYC] were getting richer and the friable middle ground where we stood was vanishing. (1940s)

Source: John Cheever. *The Stories of John Cheever*. NY: Alfred A. Knopf, 1978.

86. **G. K. (Gilbert Keith) Chesterton** (1874–1936), English author, literary critic, and journalist

I took a considerable delight in the dancing illuminations of Broadway—in Broadway. Everything there is suitable to them, the vast interminable thoroughfare, the topping houses, the dizzy and restless spirit of the whole city [NYC]. It is a city of dissolving views, and one may almost say a city of everlasting dissolution. (1922)

Source: G. K. Chesterton. *What I Saw in America*. NY: Dodd, Mead & Co., 1923.

87. **Lydia Child** (1802–1880), American author and editor, abolitionist

I see not merely uncouth grabs, and fantastic, flickering lights, of lurid hue, like a trampling troop of gnomes—but straightway my mind is filled with thoughts about mutual helpfulness, human sympathy, the common bond of brotherhood, and the mysteriously deep foundations on which society rests; or rather, on which it now reels and totters. (1843)

Note: Thoughts inspired by NYC
Source: Lydia Child. *Letters from New York* (vol. 1). NY: C. S. Francis & Co, 1843.

88. **Agatha Christie** (1891–1976), English writer, detective novels

It is ridiculous to set a detective story in New York City. New York City is itself a detective story. (1956)

Source: *Life*. May 14, 1956.

89. **Craig Claiborne** (1920–nda), American author and critic, specialized in cuisines and cookbooks

[T]he food of the city's [NYC] most celebrated dining

salons, with one perhaps two exceptions, is neither predictably elegant nor superb. More often than not it is predictably common place. (1963)

Source: *New York Times*. September 1, 1963.

90. **Gerald Bryan Clarke** (1937–   ), American author

The skyline itself was romantic: the flat-roofed glass sky-scraper had yet to be erected, and Manhattan was still an is-land of grand and ebullient architectural fantasies—minarets, ziggurats, domes, pyramids and spires. Banks resembled cathedrals, office buildings masqueraded as palaces, and spike-topped towers unabashedly vied for a place in the clouds. (1988)

Source: Gerald Clarke. *Capote: A Biography*. NY: Simon & Schuster, 1988.

91. **John Clementis** (1916–   ), American author and editor, books on various states

. . . New York City sits bold and beautiful, brash and boun-teous, a Big Apple, representing the best the country and people have to offer. Never has there been a city like it, nor will there be again. . . . It's a city of achievers, often beset by adversity, but never bested by circumstances. (1989)

Source: John Clementis. *New York Facts: A Comprehensive Look at New York Today*. Dallas: Clemens Research, 1989.

92. **Stephen Grover Cleveland** (1837–1908), American states-man, and twice U.S. President, 1885–89, and 1893–97

We will not forget that Liberty has made here her home, nor shall her chosen altar be neglected. Willing votaries will constantly keep alive its fires and these shall gleam upon the shores of our sister Republic in the East. Reflected thence and joined with answering rays, a stream of light shall pierce the darkness of ignorance and man's oppression until Liberty enlightens the world. (1886)

Note: Speech made in 1886 by President Cleveland, acceptance of Statue of Liberty as a gift from France (Sister Republic of the East).
Source: *Bearer of a Million Dreams: The Biography of the Statue of Liberty.* Ottawa, IL: Jameson Books, 1986.

93. **Florence Coates** (1850–1927), American poet

New York (A Nocturne) (poem)
How beautiful is this
Unmatched Cosmopolis!
City of wealth and want,
   Of pitiless extremes,
   Selfish ambitions, pure
     aspiring dreams. . . . (1898)

Source: Hamilton Fish Armstrong, ed. *The Book of New York's Verse.* NY: G. P. Putnam's Sons, 1917.

94. **George Cohan** (1878–1942), American actor, dramatist, and producer

Give My Regards to Broadway (song)
Give my regards to Broadway,
Remember me to Herald Square.
Tell all the gang at Forty Second Street
That I'll soon be there. (1904)

Source: *Better Homes and Gardens Family Songbook.* NY: Meredith Corp., 1975.

95. **William Cole** (1919–   ), American author and poet

New York is a great city to live in if you can afford to get out of it. (1992)

Source: William Cole. *New York: A Literary Companion*. NY: Pushcart, 1992.

96. **Emilio Colombo** (1920–   ), Italian lawyer and politician, Prime Minister of Italy, 1970–1974

Two hundred years ago Samuel Johnson wrote that anyone who had not seen Rome was really inferior. I'd like to reverse this and say there is a certain inferiority accruing to someone who has not been to New York. (1971)

Source: *New York Times*. February 23, 1971.

97. **Jesus Colon** (1901–1974), Puerto Rican-American author, poet, and short-story writer

Years ago it was "the brutal and uncouth Irish"; then it was the "knife-wielding" Italians; later it was the "clannish" Jews with "strange" ways; yesterday it was the Negro; today it is the Puerto Ricans—and the Negroes—who are relegated to the last rung of New York's social ladder. (1961)

Source: Jesus Colon. *A Puerto Rican in New York and Other Sketches*. NY: International Publishers, 1982.

98. **Calvin Colton** (1789–1857), American author, lived many years in England

Never let the poor and destitute emigrant stop at New York—it will be his ruin. (1832)

Note: Fortunately, very few immigrants took the author's advice, making New York a multiethnic/multicultural city.

Source: Calvin Colton. *Manual for the Emigrants in America.* London: F. Westley & Davis, 1832.

99. **George Combe** (1788–1858), English author, essayist, and phrenologist

The first aspect of the city on the side of the East River strikingly resembles that of Amsterdam. High, irregular, red brick fabrics, with innumerable masts, extending over a space of two miles in length, and half shading the houses from the eye, characterise both. (1841)

Source: George Combe. *Notes on the United States of America During a Phrenological Visit in 1838–1840.* Edinburgh: MacLachlin, Stewart, 1848.

100. **Richard Condon** (1915–   ), American author, fiction

Broadway was controlled by strange looking pedestrians, people who had grabbed the wrong face in the dark when someone shouted "Fire!" and were now out roaming the streets, desperate to find their own. (1959)

Source: Richard Condon. *The Manchurian Candidate.* NY: McGraw-Hill, 1959.

101. **Cyril Connolly** (1903–1974), English critic and writer

To the visiting non-competitive European all [NYC] is unending delight. The shops, the bars, the women, the faces in the street, the excellent and innumerable restaurants . . . a place where one can buy a book or meet a friend at any hour of the day or night, where every language is spoken and xenophobia almost unknown, where every purse and appetite is catered for, where every street with every quarter and the people who inhabit them are fulfilling their function, not slipping back into apathy, indifference, decay. (1947)

Source: Cyril Connolly. *Ideas and Places.* NY: Harper & Row, 1953.

102. **Peter Conrad** (1948–   ), Australian author and critic

New York is more now than the sum of its people and buildings. It makes sense only as a mechanical intelligence, a transporter system for the daily absorbing and nightly redeploying of the human multitudes whose services it requires. (1984)

Source: Peter Conrad. *The Art of the City: Views and Versions of New York.* NY: Oxford University Press, 1984.

103. **Alistair Cooke** (1908–   ), American, British-born essayist, broadcaster, and journalist

New York is the biggest collection of villages in the world. (1952)

Source: Alistair Cooke. *One Man's America.* NY: Alfred Knopf, 1952.

104. **Hope Cooke** (1940–   ), American author

In the eyes of some of my friends, most of them divorced single mothers, New York was a citadel of broken romances, each apartment building a place where something had ended—*denue,* or whatever is the opposite of *venue.* We all had internalized responses to the city's dangers and knew how to dart up empty subway stairs in case of lurkers. We also knew its special etiquettes (related to danger). (1995)

Source: Hope Cooke. *Seeing New York: History Walks for Arm Chair and Footloose Travelers.* Philadelphia: Temple University Press, 1995.

105. **James Fenimore Cooper** (1789–1851), American novelist and essayist

It is only necessary to sit down with a minute map of the country before you to perceive at a glance, that Nature herself has intended the Island of Manhattan for the site of one of the greatest commercial towns of the world. (1820)

Source: Robert E. Spiller. *Fenimore Cooper: Critic of His Time.* NY: Russell & Russell, 1963.

◆ ◆ ◆

You will find that New York possesses the advantage of a capacious and excellent roadstead, a vast harbour, an unusually extensive natural basin, with two outlets to the sea, and a river that in itself, might contain all the shipping of the earth. (1826)

Source: Fenimore Cooper. *Notions of the Americans: Picked Up by a Travelling Bachelor.* London: C. Holburn, 1828.

106. **Thomas Cooper** (1759–1839), American scientist and educator, President of South Carolina College (1821–1833)

New York, for instance, is a perfect counterpart of Liverpool; the situation of the docks, the form of the streets, the state of the public buildings, the inside as well as the outside of the public houses, the manners, the amusements, the mode of living among the expensive part of the inhabitants — all these circumstances are as nearly alike. . . . (1794)

Source: Thomas Cooper. *Some Information Respecting America.* London: D. Johnson, 1795.

107. **Sir Noël Coward** (1899–1973), English actor, playwright, and composer

I like New York in June, how about you? It is, of course, still May but I like New York in May too. In fact I like New York period. It is stimulating and busy and the apartment is charming. . . . (1957)

Source: Sir Noël Coward. *The Noël Coward Diaries* (ed. by Graham Payn and Sheridan Morley). London: Weidenfeld and Nicolson, 1982.

108. **Malcolm Cowley** (1898–1968), American author, literary critic, poet, editor, and reviewer

New York has enveloped itself for me in a haze of ragtime tunes, a sort of poetry which leads me to a melancholic happiness. To work in an office is a refuge. . . . (1923)

Source: Thomas Daniel. *Conversations with Malcolm Cowley.* Jackson, MS: University Press of Mississippi, 1986.

◆ ◆ ◆

I learned to write book reviews because when I was so poor in New York City, in the twenties, book reviews were the only thing I could get paid for. I didn't get paid very much, but, still I was paid something. . . . But since chance more or less had dictated that form to me, then, as with anybody else, I began pouring all of myself into that form and it became my sonnet sequence. (1920s)

Source: *The Selected Correspondence of Kenneth Burke and Malcolm Cowley, 1915–1981* (ed. by Paul Jay). NY: Viking Press, 1988.

109. **Henry Cramer** (1876–1930), American author, singer, and composer

Bronx Express (song)
The Bronx express brings happiness

To mother and brothers and others too
Each crowded train brings home again
Some laddie or daddy when work is thru . . . (1922)

> *Note: Music by Billy Jim Layton (1924–); the song was devoted to the Bronx express subway train.*
> Source: NYPL, Lincoln Center for the Performing Arts Library, Item 1922, Vol. 25/A.

110. **Quentin Crisp** (1908–), British author

In Manhattan, every flat is a potential stage and every inattentive waiter an unemployed, possibly unemployable, actor. (1991)

> Source: *New Statesman & Society* (British publication). August 9, 1991.

111. **David (Davy) Crockett** (1786–1836), American frontiersman and politician

A bulger of a place it [NYC] is. The number of the ships beat me a hollow, and looked for all the world like a big clearing in the West, with the dead trees all standing. (1835)

> Source: David Crockett. *An Account of Col. Crockett's Tour to the North and Down East Written by Himself.* Philadelphia: E. L. Corey & A. Hart, 1835.

112. **E. E. (Edward Estlin) Cummings** (1894–1962), American poet

[NYC is] the sensual mysticism of entire vertical being. (1920s)

> Source: *Architectural Digest.* September 1986.

113. **Bloodgood H. Cutter** (1817–1906), American, New York
     City (Queens)-born poet

     On Laying the Corner Stone of the Town Hall
     at Flushing, L. I. (poem), 1862
     This may be entirely small,
     Then build one like City Hall;
     Perhaps for a market, this will take,
     Then in it alterations make
     When they open this corner stone,
     They'll scan these relics, ev'ryone
     And when each piece comes to their view,
     They'll judge us, of 1862

     Note: Flushing is a section of Queens Borough in NYC.
     Source: Bloodgood E. Cutter. *The Long Island Farmer's Poems.*
        NY: Tibbas, 1886.

114. **Salvador Dali** (1904–1989), Spanish, Catalan-born, surreal-
     ist painter

     New York, you are an Egypt! But an Egypt turned inside out.
     For she erected pyramids of slavery to death, and you erect
     pyramids of democracy with the vertical organpipes of your
     skyscrapers all meeting at the point of infinity of liberty!
     (1942)

     Source: Salvador Dali. *The Secret Life of Salvador Dali* (transl.
        from the French by Haakon Chevalier). NY: Dial Press, 1942.

115. **Raphael D'Amour** (1860–1931), French poet, often visited
     NYC

     A Modern Odyssey (poem)
     I sing, O Muse, a most amazing thing—
     That even wreathed Homer could not sing
     An Epic of the Underground . . .

One neighbor, arms about my shoulders surled,
Crams down my throat a copy of the *World,*
Three other neighbors angrily compete
To see which one shall walk upon my feet
All, all munch gum. . . . (1929)

*Note: Author's impressions after riding the subway from the Bronx
to Brooklyn*
Source: *New York* (magazine). July 1929. (Magazine is out of print
and is not related to the current *New York Magazine* that has
been published since 1968.)

116. **Leopold Damrosch** (1832–1885), American musician, inventor of color photography

New York with its hustle and bustle is the cosmopolitan city
PAR EXCELLENCE with no room for narrowmindedness.
I find the uneasing activity of the city very attractive and invigorating, something that was very much lacking in Breslau
[Poland]. . . . (1872)

*Note: The author was the father of Walter Damrosch, after whom
the park at Lincoln Center is named*
Source: George Martin. *The Damrosch Dynasty: America's First
Family of Music.* Boston: Houghton Mifflin, 1983.

117. **Tom Davies** (1940–   ), British author

She [Manhattan] has become a wicked and wild bitch in her
old age . . . but there is still no sensation in the world quite
like walking her sidewalks. Great surges of energy sweep all
around you, the air fizzes like champagne, while always
there is a nervous edge of fear and whispered distant
promises of sudden violence. (1979)

Source: *Observer Review* (British publication). November 11,
1979.

118. **Richard Harding Davis** (1864–1916), American journalist, historian, author, and playwright

    At twenty-third street . . . Broadway takes on the leisurely air, . . . this is the most interesting spot in the city to the stranger in our gates, and it is, after all, that we all know and like the best. It is so cosmopolitan, so alive, and so rich in color and monument, and so generous in its array of celebrities. . . . One could wear a turban here, or a pith helmet, or a sealskin ulster down to heels, and his passing would cause no comment. (1892)

    Source: Richard H. Davis. *The Great Streets of the World.* NY: Charles Scribner's Sons, 1892.

119. **Charles de Gaulle** (1890–1970), French general, President of France from 1945 to 1946, and from 1959 to 1969

    There is and has long been . . . a special bond between New York and me. . . . How often, at difficult moments, I looked to New York, I listened to New York, to find out what you were thinking and feeling here, and always I found a comforting echo. (1960)

    Note: Quoted from a speech given during a lunch honoring de Gaulle on April 26, 1960 in NYC.
    Source: *New York Times.* April 27, 1960.

120. **David Dempsey** (1914–   ), American author and journalist

    Most of them (bohemians) lead lives of unquiet desperation, continually seeking, in sex they wish was love and in love they suspect is only sex, a center for their worlds to turn on. (1958)

    Note: Reference is made to a segment of population in Greenwich Village, New York City.
    Source: *New York Times,* April 27, 1958

121. **Gabor Demszky** (1953–   ), Hungarian Mayor of Budapest and former anti-Communist dissident

Those people who left the Austro-Hungarian monarchy — from Budapest, Prague, Vienna — they built New York City. In New York you see the same buildings, the same architecture. It has the same feeling. Here (Budapest) we have a multicultural atmosphere. . . . Yet we have illiteracy, criminality, drugs, terror. All these things give us a similarity [with NYC]. (1995)

Note: Author lived in NYC in the 1980s
Source: *New York Times*. February 27, 1995.

122. **Charles Dickens** (1812–1870), English novelist

Debauchery [in Five Points] has made the very houses prematurely old. See how the rotten beams are tumbling down, and how the patched and broken windows seem to scowl dimly, like eyes that have been hurt in drunken frays. Many of those pigs live here. Do they ever wonder why their masters walk upright in lieu of going on all-fours? and why they talk instead of grunting? (1842)

Note: Five Points was a notorious poverty- and crime-ridden section in nineteenth-century NYC.
Source: Charles Dickens. *American Notes*. NY: St. Martin's Press, 1985 (reprint of 1842 edition).

123. **Joan Didion** (1935–   ), American author and essayist

New York is full of people . . . with a feeling for the tangential adventure, the risky adventure, the interlude that's not likely to end in a double-ring ceremony. (1961)

Source: *Mademoiselle*. February 1961.

◆ ◆ ◆

It is often said that New York is a city for only the very rich and the very poor. It is less often said that New York is also, at least for those of us who came there from somewhere else, a city for only the very young. (1967)

Source: Joan Didion. *Slouching Towards Bethlehem.* New York: Farrar, Straus & Giroux, 1968.

124. **David Dinkins** (1927–), African American politician, NYC Mayor from 1990 to 1993

New York is a city of throbbing vitality—a metropolis alive with the sights and sounds of its many diverse neighborhoods. I often describe New York as a mosaic, a rich quilt of many patches, colors, and sizes, each piece distinct, yet their whole bound together by a common thread. (1986)

Source: Peter A. Bailey and Edith J. Slade. *Harlem Today: A Cultural and Visitor's Guide.* NY: Gumbs and Thomas, 1986 (introduction).

◆ ◆ ◆

As a boy in Harlem, I and many of my friends saw Columbia [University] as a gateway to opportunity and hope. Columbia still provides those same elusively essential ingredients for our city and for the international community as well. (1994)

Source: *Columbia: The Magazine of Columbia University.* Fall 1994.

125. **John Dos Passos** (1896–1970), American novelist

I think this city is full of people wanting inconceivable things. (1925)

Source: John Dos Passos. *Manhattan Transfer*. Cambridge, MA: R. Bentley, 1980 (reprint of earlier editions).

126. **Theodore Dreiser** (1871–1945), American novelist and magazine editor

The thing that impressed then as now about New York . . . was the sharp, and at the same time immense, contrast it showed between the dull and the shrewd, the strong and the week, the rich and the poor, the wise and the ignorant. . . . [T]hose who ultimately dominated were so very strong, and the weak so very, very weak—and so very, very many. (1923)

Source: Theodore Dreiser. *The Color of a Grey City*. NY: Bone and Liveright, 1923.

127. **Paul Lawrence Dunbar** (1872–1906), African American poet, short story writer, and novelist

To the provincial coming to New York for the first time, ignorant and unknown, the city presents a notable mingling of cheerness [sic] and gloom. If he has any eye at all for the beautiful, he cannot help experiencing a thrill as he crosses the ferry over the river filled with playing craft, and catches the first sight of the spires and buildings of New York. . . . [I]f he be a fool . . . the Bowery will be his romance, Broadway his lyric, and the Park his pastoral and he will look down pityingly on all the rest of humanity. (1902)

Source: Paul Lawrence Dunbar. *The Sports of the Gods*. Miami, FL: Mnemosque Publishing, 1993 (reprint from 1902 edition).

128. **Dominick Dunne** (1925–   ) American author and screenplay writer

The best thing about New York is that you can never know it all, no matter how long you live here. The worst thing is that it's no longer safe to walk and wander around different parts of this city. There is always a need to look over your shoulder to make sure there is no one behind you. (1993)

Source: *New York* (magazine). December 20–27, 1993.

129. **Finley Peter Dunne** (1867–1936), American humorist

Nearly all th' most foolish people in th' country and minny iv th' wisest goes to Noo York. Th' wise people ar-re there because th' foolish wint first. That's th' way th' wise men make a livin.' (1901)

Source: Finley Peter Dunne. *Mr. Dooley's Opinions*. NY: R. H. Russell, 1901.

130. **John Gregory Dunne** (1932–), American author

New York is at once cosmopolitan and parochial, a compendium of sentimental certainties. It is in fact the most sentimental of the world's great cities—in its selfcongratulation a kind of San Francisco of the East. (1977)

Source: John G. Dunne. *True Confessions: A Novel*. NY: Dutton, 1977.

131. **Ernest Duvergier de Hauranne** (1843–77) French writer and politician

The first impression of New York is that it is repulsive and vulgar. The broken pavements, the muddy streets, the squares overrun with grass and underbrush, the disreputable horse cars, and the irregular houses plastered with huge hand-bills have the careless ugliness of an open-air bazaar. The old cities of Europe all have character. This has nothing but commonplaceness. . . . (1864)

Source: Ernest Duvergier de Hauranne. *Huit Mois en Amerique: Lettres et Notes de Voyage, 1864–1865 (Eight Months in America: Voyage Letters and Notes, 1864–1865)*. Paris: A. Lacroix, Verboeckhoven, 1866 (title and quotation translated from the French).

132. **Thomas T. Eaton** (1845–1907), American poet and author

Describing View of New York (poem)
. . .
Broadway the first to take the eye,
The noblest street I here espy,
The new-swept side walks neat and clean,
With poplars shaded sweet and green,
And sev'ral thousand stylish folks
Are seen repassing on the walks (1873)

Source: Hamilton Fish Armstrong, ed. *The Book of New York's Verse*. NY: G. P. Putnam's Sons, 1917.

133. **Edward Robb Ellis** (1911–   ), American historian and author

They came in a great ship. There were 110 men, women and children, representing thirty families and they arrived in "New Amsterdam", a vessel of unusual size for that age — (displacing 260 tons). . . . [T]he man who brought them to America was . . . Cornelis Jacobsen May . . . first director of New Netherland after it had been declared a Dutch province. (1966)

Note: Refers to the arrival of first Dutch colonists in Manhattan in May 1623.
Source: Edward Robb Ellis. *The Epic of New York City*. NY: Coward-McCann, 1966.

134. **Ralph Ellison** (1914–   ), African American author

Then at the street intersection I had the shock of seeing a black policeman directing traffic—and there were white drivers who obeyed his signals as though it was the most natural thing in the world. . . . This really was Harlem. (1947)

> *Note: First impressions of the narrator coming to New York for the first time from the South.*
> Source: Ralph Ellison. *The Invisible Man*. NY: Random House, 1952.

135. **Ralph Waldo Emerson** (1803–1882), American poet, essayist, and philosopher

For a national, for an imperial prosperity, everything here [NYC] seems irrevocably destined. What a Bay! What a River! What climate. What men! . . . What manners, what histories and poetry shall rapidly arise and for how long, and, it seems, endless date! . . . But in my next transfiguration, I think I should choose New York. (1840)

> Source: Ralph L. Rusk. *The Life of Ralph Waldo Emerson*. NY: Charles Scribner's Sons, 1949.

136. **William Emerson, Jr.** (1943–   ), American author

New York is the greatest city in the world for lunch. . . . That's the gregarious time. And when that first Martini hits the liver like a silver bullet, there is a sigh of contentment that can be heard in Dubuque. (1975)

> Source: *Newsweek*. December 29, 1975.

137. **Evan Esar** (1899–NDA), American author, quotations compiler

New Yorkers rush by the day to save time they will waste at

night. . . . Traffic is so slow in New York that the taxi meters run faster than the taxicabs. (1968)

Source: Evan Esar. *20,000 Quips and Quotes*. NY: Doubleday & Co, 1968.

138. **Oriana Fallaci** (1930–   ), Italian author

I'm going to show you the real New York—witty, smart, and international—like any metropolis. Tell me this—where in Europe can you find old Hungary, old Russia, old France, old Italy? In Europe you're trying to copy America, you're almost American. But here you'll find Europeans who immigrated a hundred years ago and we haven't spoiled them. Oh, Gio! You must see why I love New York. Because the whole world's in New York. (1966)

Source: Oriana Fallaci. *Penelope at War* (translated from the Italian by Pamela Swinglehurst). London: M. Joseph, 1966.

139. **Bernard Faÿ** (1893–NDA), French author and historian

New York is constructed to the scale of the United States, as Athens was built for the Greek Republic, and Paris for the kingdom of France. The very thing that I admire most in New York is its adaptation to the continent. In this sense, its architecture is intellectually reasonable, logical and beautiful. Skyscrapers are the dwellings of the supertrusts; they are Eiffel tower cathedrals which shelter Mr. Rockefeller, the emperor of Petroleum. . . . (1929)

Source: Bernard Faÿ. *The American Experiment*. Port Washington, NY: Kennikat Press, 1969 (reprint of 1929 ed.).

140. **James Felt** (1903–   ), Chairman of the City Planning Administration (NYC) in 1970s

The greatest humanitarian movements have been born here or have found a home here, from child care to the United Nations. There are miracles here everywhere; there is the continuing miracle of redevelopment—and yet there is always room for more great things to come. (1971)

Source: *New York Times*. March 5, 1971.

141. **Nat Ferber** (1899–1945), American author

The Jew in Brownsville thinks that he alone is living in New York . . . and the Italian of East Twelfth Street thinks that his little Italy is all of New York. And the same goes for the German and the Irishman who looks upon everybody else, coming from a district peculiar to his kind, as an alien. What none of them realize is that it took all their districts, each a foreign country, to make this city what it is. (1919)

Source: Nat Ferber. *New York: A Novel*. NY: Covici-Friede Publishers, 1919.

142. **Rudolph Fisher** (1897–1934), African American short story writer

. . . Negroes at every turn, up and down Lenox Avenue and up and down 135th Street; big, lanky Negroes, short squat Negroes; black ones, brown ones, yellow ones; men standing idle on the curb; women, bunded-laden, trudging reluctantly homeward, children rattle-trapping about sidewalks; here and there a white face drifting along, but Negroes predominantly, overwhelmingly everywhere. . . . This was Negro Harlem. (1925)

Source: Rudolph Fisher. *The City of Refuge: Collected Stories*. Columbia, MO: University of Missouri Press, 1987.

143. **Trevor Fishlock** (1941–), English author

New York is a city of strong flavours, of gasps and not sighs. It feeds you on mustard and tabasco sauce and makes you mainline on adrenalin. It is not possible to be neutral about it. It has a thumping heart. . . . Almost everything you have heard about it is largely true. (1980)

Source: Trevor Fishlock. *Americans and Nothing Else.* London: Cassell, 1980.

144. **F. Scott Fitzgerald** (1896–1940), American novelist

I began to like New York, the racy, adventurous feel of it at night, and the satisfaction that the constant flicker of men and women and machines gives to the restless eye. . . . The city seen from the Queensboro Bridge is always the city seen for the first time, in its first wild promise of all the mystery and beauty in the world. (1925)

Source: F. Scott Fitzgerald. *The Great Gatsby.* NY: Charles Scribner's Sons, 1958 (reprint of 1925 ed.).

145. **Zelda Fitzgerald** (1900–1948), American author, wife of F. Scott Fitzgerald

Possessing a rapacious engulfing ego, their [New Yorkers] particular genius swallowed their world in its swift undertow and washes its cadavers out to sea. New York is a good place to be on the up-grade. (1932)

Source: Zelda Fitzgerald. *Save Me the Waltz.* Carbondale, IL: Southern Illinois University Press, 1932.

146. **Ford Madox Ford** (1873–1939), English poet and author

New York differs from London in having a keener intellectual life; it differs from Paris in that intellectual circles are smaller. Perhaps the products of the intellect are less valued here by the bulk of the people than it is the case in other cities—but New York is becoming more and more of an intellectual center as the days go on—and that adds enormously to the world. (1926)

Source: Ford Madox Ford. *New York Is Not America*. London: Duckworth, 1927.

◆ ◆ ◆

Tips are of appallingly high scale in this city and must by no means be omitted if efficient attention is desired. If, however, the traveller does not intend again to visit the establishment the formality may be omitted. (1932)

Source: Ford Madox Ford. *Return to Yesterday*. NY: H. Liveright, 1932.

147. **Henry Ford** (1863–1947), American automobile manufacturer

New York is a different country. Maybe it ought to have a separate government. Everybody thinks differently, acts differently. They just don't know what the hell the rest of the United States is. (1940s)

Source: *Reader's Digest*. October 1973.

148. **Ludwig Fulda** (1862–1939), German dramatist and author

One could believe that giants had built this city for giants, and if you walk in Lower Broadway, among the monsters, you get the illusion of being in a deep mountain canyon. . . . Among the prizeworthy marvels of New York, one must not overlook its transportation system. In its layout, this too appears to have been built by giants, and it surpasses that of all European cities. (1906)

Source: Ludwig Fulda. *Amerikanische Eindruke (American Impressions)*. Stuttgart/Berlin: J. Kota, 1914 (title and quotation translated from the German).

149. **Buckminster Fuller** (1895–1983), American architect, engineer and author

I've walked over the Brooklyn Bridge many times, and I've always felt impressed by it. I used to make it my cathedral, the place where I could get close to the Almighty. Now I'm able to get taller than the buildings in my thinking. (1971)

Source: *New York Times*. March 13, 1971.

150. **John K. Galbraith** (1908–   ), American (Canadian-born) economist and author

Once the visitor was told rather repetitively that this city was the melting pot; never before in history had so many people of such varied languages, customs, colors and culinary habits lived so amicably together. Although New York remains peaceful by most standards, this selfcongratulation is now less often heard, since it was discovered some years ago that racial harmony depended unduly on the willingness of Blacks (and lately Puerto Ricans) to do for the other races the meanest jobs at the lowest wages. . . . (1971)

Source: John Galbraith. *View from the Stands: Of People, Politics, Military Power and the Arts*. Boston: Houghton Mifflin, 1986 (reprint of earlier articles).

151. **Federico García Lorca** (1898–1936), Spanish poet and playwright

New York is a meeting place for every race in the world, but the Chinese, Armenians, Russians, and Germans remain foreigners. So does everyone except the blacks. There is no doubt that the blacks exercise great influence in North America, and, no matter what anyone says, they are the most delicate, spiritual element in the world. (1931)

Source: Federico García Lorca. *Poet in New York* (transl. from the Spanish by Ben Belitt). NY: Grove Press, 1983 (original text published in 1940).

152. **Vincent Gardenia** (1923–1992), American television and theater actor

Because of the great influx of Italians to New York, Italian theater, in the various dialects, offered an inexpensive distraction from the hard life the immigrants found in their new country. There were . . . theater troups acting in the Sicilian and Calabrese dialects, for instance, but my father's troup was known as the best company that performed in the Neapolitan tongue. (1920s)

Source: Ralph Monti. *I Remember Brooklyn: Memoirs from Famous Sons and Daughters*. NY: Carol Publishing, 1991.

153. **Stephen Garmey** (1933–   ), American author, topic: NYC architecture

Today the Park (Gramercy) seems almost a mirage-like London Square of a hundred years ago—with graceful trees, shady lawns, cast-iron gates, and flagstone sidewalks. The fine brick houses on the West Side are almost as beautiful as when they were built in the 1840's. (1984)

Note: Gramercy Park is a section in the Lower West Side of Manhattan.
Source: Stephen Garmey. *Gramercy Park: An Illustrated History of a New York Neighborhood.* NY: Balsam Press, 1984.

154. **Joel Garreau** (1948–   ), American educator and author

It never occured to him [a New Yorker] that New York might be a bad idea, that it might be caving in under the artificiality of its existence. What was life without a thousand Chinese restaurants? (1981)

Source: Joel Garreau. *The Nine Nations of North America.* Boston: Houghton Mifflin, 1981.

155. **Crosbie Garstin** (1887–1930), American author and illustrator

New York is a good spot to stop away from. (1928)

Note: Garstin wrote this on the eve of the Great Depression.
Source: Crosbie Garstin. *The Dragon and the Lotus.* NY: F. A. Stokes, 1927.

156. **William Geist** (1945–   ), American author

New York is a city of conversations overheard, of people at the next restaurant table (micrometers away) checking your watch, of people reading the stories in your newspaper on the subway train, a quiet standoff at the barbershop. (1986)

Source: *New York Times.* October 25, 1986.

157. **Henry George** (1839–1897), American economist and reformer

The upper part of New York [City] is a beautiful place—the streets wide, clear and regular; the houses all a brownstone and standing ten or twenty feet from the pavements with gardens in front. . . . The view from this spot [The Battery] is beautiful—the North River and the New York Bay covered with sailing vessels and steamers of every class and size, while back, the hills gently sloping, are covered with country seats. . . . (1855)

Source: Henry George. *The Life of Henry George*. Garden City, NY: Doubleday, Doran & Co., 1930.

158. **Walter Lionel George** (1882–1926), English journalist and novelist

One goes up Broadway at night to see crowded colored signs of the movie shows and the theatres twinkle and eddy, inviting, glamorous, Babylonian! You see all the great cities of the present and the past come into my mind and make my judgement fantastic. For New York is all the cities. (1920)

Source: Walter Lionel George. *Hail Columbia: Random Impressions of a Conservative English Radical*. NY/London: Harper Brothers, 1921.

159. **Richard Watson Gilder** (1844–1909), American poet and editor

The City (poem)
City of glorious days,
    Of hope, and labor and mirth,
With room and to spare, only thy splendid bays,
    For the ships of all earth! (1908)

Note: Poem devoted to NYC
Source: Richard Watson Gilder. *The Poems of Richard Watson Gilder*. Boston: Houghton Mifflin, 1908.

160. **Brendan Gill** (1914–), American author and journalist

New York is thought to be a city that continuously, reck-lessly throws itself down and builds itself up again in the course of a century. . . . But in fact there are many sections of the city where nearly everything one looks upon has re-mained contentedly in place for generations. . . . (1990)

Note: Reference is made to the Algonguin Hotel (built in 1901) and many other landmark buildings.
Source: Brendan Gill. *A New York Life: Of Friends and Others.* NY: Poseidon Press, 1990.

◆ ◆ ◆

Though the avenues of New York are justly admired by vis-itors from all over the world, local citizens are inclined to prefer its sidestreets . . . mine is West Forty-Fourth, where nearly every day for over half a century I have been part of the ebb and flow of its tides of pedestrians, whether early in the morning . . . or late at night when pyramids of black plas-tic trashbags are piled on the curb in hillocks that reach higher than my head. (1990)

Source: Brendan Gill. *A New York Life: Of Friends and Others.* NY: Poseidon Press, 1990.

161. **Charlotte Perkins Gilman** (1860–1935), American author

New York . . . that natural city where every one is in exile, none more so than the American. (1935)

Source: Charlotte Perkins Gilman. *The Living of Charlotte Perkins Gilman: An Autobiography.* Madison, WI: University of Wis-consin Press, 1991 (reprint of 1935 edition).

162. **Allen Ginsberg** (1926–), American poet of the Beat gen-eration

So you walk down the city streets in New York for a few blocks, you get this gargantuan feeling of buildings. You walk all day you'll be at the verge of tears. More detail, more attention to the significance of all that robotic detail that impinges on the mind and you realize through your own bodies fears that you are surrounded by a giant robot machine which is crushing and separating people, removing them from nature and removing them from living and dying. (1974)

Source: Allen Ginsberg. *The Craft of Poetry: Interviews from the New York Quarterly* (ed. by William Packard). New York: Doubleday, 1974.

163. **Eli Ginzberg** (1911–), American author and university professor

New York is unique, in that it has the whole world linked to it. The problems, particularly racial ones, seem overconcentrated here now, but that won't last forever. It would take more ineptitude than past or present politicians have shown to ruin the city. (1971)

Source: *New York Times*. April 30, 1971.

164. **Rudolph Giuliani** (1944–), American lawyer, politician and NYC Mayor 1994–97

If you come here [NYC] and you work hard and you happen to be in an undocumented status [alien], you are one of the people who we want in this city. You are somebody that we want to protect and we want you to get out from under what is often the life of being like a fugitive, which is really unfair. (1994)

Source: *New York Times*. October 4, 1994.

165. **Malcolm Gladwell** (1963–   ), American journalist

In New York, no young woman can reliably screen her list of potential suitors insisting on Democratic Party membership because that label covers everyone from Irish cops in Staten Island to West Indian immigrants in Brooklyn to Fukienese shopkeepers in Chinatown to Dominican cabdrivers in the Bronx to hardened East Village leather-wearing radicals to do-gooding banker's sons on the Upper East Side. Unless her tastes were unusually indiscriminate, she would eventually just throw up her hands. (1994)

Source: *Washington Post Magazine*. November 6, 1994.

166. **Anka Godjevac-Subbotich** (1908?–   ), Serbian American lawyer, diplomat, and author

Everything in New York except for its skyscrapers and its pace is a replica of the Old World. New York is the last stop coming from Europe and the first upon entering America. Manhattan is like an oxygen tent for us Europeans, who parachuted to this new way of living and this New World, after having lost all meaningful and valuable assets, our homeland and our name. Sometimes when sentimental nostalgia for Europe asphyxiates, breathing in the air of this European replica makes one feel better. (1961)

Source: Anka Godjevac-Subbotich. *From Three Continents*. Melbourne: Self-published, 1961 (title and quotation translated from the Serbian).

167. **Michael Gold** (1894–1967), American author, Jewish topics

New York is a devil's dream, the most urbanized city in the world. It is all geometry angles and stone. It is mythical, a city buried by a volcano. No grass is found in this petrified city, no big living trees, no flowers, no bird, but the drab little lecherous sparrow, no soil, loam, earth, fresh earth to smell, earth to walk on, to roll on, and love like a woman. (1930)

Source: Michael Gold. *Jews Without Money*. NY: Avon Books, 1965 (reprint of earlier editions).

168. **Carey Goldberg** (NDA), American journalist

This season's visitors from abroad, New York's biggest year for foreign tourists so far this decade, might be compared to the blind men touching this elephant of a city. The conclusions they reach depend on what they are shown, how they are shown it and their own prisms and preconceptions. . . . Tourism officials estimate that more than two million foreign tourists have visited New York this summer, more than the number of immigrants that came through Ellis Island in any year of peak immigration. (1995)

Source: *New York Times,* August 21, 1995.

169. **Paul Goldberger** (1941–), American author and architecture critic

New York remains what it has always been: a city of ebb and flow, a city of constant shifts of population and economics, a city of virtually no rest. It is harsh, dirty, and dangerous, it is whimsical and fanciful, it is beautiful and new, the large, the prosperous, the fashionable. (1979)

Source: Paul Goldberger. *The City Observed: New York*. NY: Random House, 1979.

◆ ◆ ◆

Nowhere else in New York does God confront Mammon as directly as where Trinity Church meets Wall Street. A landmark Gothic Revival church staring down the canyon of capitalism: what better way for architecture to symbolize the very conflict of urban civilization? (1996)

Note: The Trinity Church, 281 feet high, is celebrating its 150th anniversary; the original building, erected in 1697 and destroyed by fire in 1753, was replaced by a second building in 1790 (which was destroyed in 1839 by a storm and snowfall), and it was finally replaced by a third building in 1846.
Source: *New York Times,* May 14, 1996, pp. B1–B2.

170. **Harris (Harry) Golden** (1903–1981), American, NYC born author and critic, Jewish topics

Within its limits, New York City has more Jews than have ever congregated in a single city in the history of the world. . . . It is a Jewish city because the attitudes, culture, art, theaters, stores, fashions, music, writing, television and most of the producers and directors, artists and architects are Jewish. (1972)

Source: Harris (Harry) Golden. *The Greatest Jewish City in the World.* Garden City, NY: Doubleday & Co., 1972.

171. **Jonathan Goldman** (1944–   ), American author

If to a child the Empire State [Building] has some of the qualities of an oversized toy, to an adult it is inevitably a symbol—an icon, at the very least, of New York City. While the Statue of Liberty stands for the dream of New York as the safe haven at the end of every immigrant's wanderings, the Empire State says something about the power and the style of the town. It has to do with the machine, much to do with business, and still more to do with elegance and pride. (1980)

Source: Jonathan Goldman. *The Empire State Building Book.* NY: St. Martin's Press, 1980.

172. **Roy Goodman** (1930–   ), American politician, NYS Senator

Prostitution is the only business that isn't leaving the city. (1976)

Note: Quotation from a speech delivered to the New York Press Club on October 24, 1976.
Source: *New York Times*. October 25, 1976.

173. **Maxim Gorky** (1868–1936), Russian novelist, playwright, and critic

Twenty-storied houses, dark soundless skyscrapers stand on the shore [of NYC]. Square, lacking in any desire to be beautiful, the bulky, ponderous buildings tower gloomily and drearily. A haughty pride in its height, and its ugliness is felt in each house. There are no flowers in the window, and no children to be seen. . . . From this distance the city seems like a vast saw with black teeth. It breathes clods of black smoke into the sky and puffs like a glutton suffering from obesity. (1906)

Source: *Appleton's Magazine*. Vol. 8, 1906 (author's article included).

174. **Nigel Gosling** (1909–1982), American author, dance and art critic

New York is a granite beehive, where people jostle and whir like molecules in an overheated jar. . . . (1967)

Source: *Saturday Review*. October 7, 1967.

175. **Heywood "Woody" Gould** (1942–   ), American, NYC-born author

It was early June and New York was already a ghost town. The rich had departed at the first sign of a Puerto Rican with a transistor. Politicians hung in to turn on a few fire hydrants and pose with some wet Third Worlders before taking off on junkets that kept them away until Labor Day. . . . The rest of the population scrambled for exits like people in a burning theater. The five million or so who remained . . . were either poor, or maladroit or too gauche to get away. A city full of pariahs. And they knew it. (1981)

Source: Heywood Gould. *Glitterburn*. NY: St. Martin's. Press, 1981.

176. **William Goyen** (1945–   ), American author, composer, and poet

I presently live in a large apartment on the West Side of New York City. One of those rooms is mine, and it's an absolute hideaway, yet all around me in the other rooms, the life of the family goes on. . . . I also like to know that twelve flights down I can step onto the street in the midst of a lot of human beings and feel a part of those. . . . Maybe solitude is best had in the midst of multitudes. (1975)

Source: George Plimpton, ed. *Writers at Work: The Paris Review Interviews*. NY: Penguin Books, 1984 (6th series).

177. **Dick Gregory** (1932–   ), African American actor, political activist, and author

New York is the greatest city in the world—especially for my people. Where else, in this grand and glorious land of ours, can I get on a subway, sit in any part of the train I please, get off at any station above 110th Street, and know I'll be welcome? (1962)

Source: Dick Gregory. *From the Back of the Bus*. NY: Avon Books, 1962.

178. **Thomas Griffith** (1915–   ), American author

Rudeness is the privacy of New Yorkers. (1956)

Source: Thomas Griffith. *The Waist-High Culture*. NY: Harper & Row, 1956.

179. **William Grimes** (1911–   ), American journalist

In the late 20th century New York, art takes its first bow in a room as loud and crowded as a commodities trading pit and as smoked-filled as an off-track betting parlor. The fruits of the genius are toasted with Chilean chardonnay and honored with offerings of suspect cheese. For a mad two hours, artists, critics, hangers-on, insiders, befuddled outsiders . . . mingle, collide, preen, dish, fawn, toady, snub and, as a last resort, take a fleeting glance at the art on the wall. . . . This ritual . . . is known as an art opening. (1995)

Source: *New York Times*. February 10, 1995.

180. **Ernest Gruening** (1887–1974), American historian and author

Courtship in New York is of necessity hurried, furtive, interrupted, irrationally exposed or confined. . . . Friendship in New York is hindered by its distances, its haste, its proprieties, its irresistible propulsion. As for casual contacts, the city's philosophy is everyone for himself. (1923)

Source: Ernest Gruening. *These United States*. Freeport, NY: Books for Libraries, 1971 (reprint of 1923 edition).

181. **Arthur Guiterman** (1871–1943), American poet, composer, and song writer

Those lions still rude and wild,

For while they pose as meek and mild,
　To keep their fierceness hid,
Down from their pedestals they'd leap,
As soon as New York went to sleep—
　If New York ever did! (1915)

Note: Reference is made to the two landmark lions in front of the
　New York Public Library, Fifth Avenue and 42nd Street. They
　were sculpted by Edward C. Potter (1857–1923), American
　sculptor.
Source: The New York Public Library. *The New York Public Li-*
　brary in Fiction, Poetry and Children's Literature. NY: New
　York Public Library, 1950.

◆　◆　◆

Collecting and publishing legends is a thankless task, at least
in a city like New York where the modern has so completely
deafened out the old that few New Yorkers realize what his-
torically interesting ground they walk upon. (1944)

Source: Arthur Guiterman. *Brave Laughter.* NY: E. P. Dutton,
　1944 (introduction).

182.　**John Gunther** (1901–1970), American historian and author

New York City, the incomparable, the brilliant star city of
cities, the forty-ninth state, a law into itself, the Cyclopedian
paradox, the inferno with no out-of-bounds, the supreme expression of both miseries and the splendors of contemporary
civilization, the Macedonia of the United States. It meets the
most severe test that may be applied to definition of metropolis—it stays up all night. But also it becomes a small town
when it rains. (1947)

Source: John Gunther. *Inside U.S.A.* New York: Harper & Row,
　1951 (reprint of 1947 edition).

183. **Tyrone Guthrie** (1900–1971), British theater director and writer

It is one of the great charms of New York that at the Met [Metropolitan Opera] one may still see bejeweled Grandes Dames, rouged like crazy, wearing what at first glance appear to be black fur stoles, but then turn out to be their enervated sons slung across their mamas' magnificent shoulders; one may still see Elderly Patricians hanging from boxes by the heels, with their opera glasses pointing like guns right *down* the décolletage of a huge soprano. . . . (1958)

Source: *New York Times Magazine.* January 5, 1958.

184. **Clyde Haberman** (NDA), American journalist

You might have noticed New York men walking with an extra bounce in their step yesterday, and the most likely reason was they'd heard the good news: fresh scientific studies show that they may be proud carriers of the highest sperm counts in the country. (1996)

Note: According to these studies, New York men have an average sperm count of 131.5 million sperm per milliliter of semen; Los Angeles men have an average count of 72.7 million sperm per milliliter of semen.
Source: *New York Times,* April 30, 1996, p. B1.

185. **Andrew Hacker** (1929–   ), American author, political topics

No single medium can convey New York. Reginald Marsh and Raphael Soyer, Leonard Bernstein and George M. Cohan—each has captured the city's cadence in a different way. A thousand movies and as many novels have shown how the rhythms of its streets shape the personality of its people. No one book can provide a full portrait. (1975)

Source: Andrew Hacker. *The New Yorkers: A Profile of an American Metropolis.* NY: Mason/Charter, 1975.

186. **Peter Halász** (1922–   ), Hungarian author and dramatist

This city [NYC] is used and abused by millions of people. . . . Cities have souls. They know how they are treated. New York got tough. The crowds do not treat her right. She is not nice to the crowds either. She is nice only to the privileged — and only for incredibly large sums of money. (1967)

Source: Peter Halász. *Second Avenue.* Toronto: Pannonia Publishers, 1967 (title and quotation translated from the Hungarian).

187. **David Halberstam** (1934–   ), American author, politics and government topics

The disadvantages of a writer living in New York are obvious. Life here is always noisy, always expensive and occasionally quite jarring . . . Yet I must admit I like living here. I stay on my own choice . . . It is my city, among other reasons, because it is a good city to be a writer in. It is home for other writers, which makes an infinitely pleasant camp for me. (1995)

Source: *New York Times,* September 9, 1995

188. **Pete Hamill** (1935–   ), American, NYC (Brooklyn)-born author and journalist

If you want to make Brooklyn in words or film or paint, you must see the way the sun defines the silent streets on an early Sunday morning, sculpting trees, buildings, fire hydrants, stray dogs, and wandering people with an almost perfect clarity. . . . If you have ever lived in Brooklyn or if you grew up on its streets, you carry that light with you forever. (1994)

Source: Andrea Wyatt Sexton and Alice Leccese Powers, eds. *The Brooklyn Reader: 30 Writers Celebrate America's Favorite Borough.* NY: Harmony Books, 1994.

189. **Mark Hampton** (1920–   ), American author

The best thing about New York is the people who live here and work here. People had told me that when they arrive here from places like Europe, they feel 10 years younger. This is the place where things get done. It's where all the activity is, and it's the starting point for a lot of creative people. (1993)

Source: *New York* (magazine). December 20–27, 1993.

190. **Helene Hanff** (1916–   ), American author and editor

No other city on earth has such a mania for tearing down the old to build the new—which I approve of. . . . My theory is that since New Yorkers mostly come here from somewhere else, they have no interest in the city's past; they come with big plans for its future. And on a narrow strip of island [Manhattan] you can't build the future without tearing down the past first, there isn't room for both. (1978)

Source: Helene Hanff. *Apple of My Eye.* Garden City, NY: Doubleday & Co., 1978.

191. **Elizabeth Hardwick** (1916–   ), American author

When you think of old New York, I, at least, don't think of the patricians, but of the Lower East Side and Harlem—both are gone, wiped out as images of promise, change, relief from the old country or from the South or whatever, as places that created styles like the jazziness of Harlem that captivated Europe and the experience of generations of immigrants. (1984)

Source: George Plimpton, ed. *Writers at Work: The Paris Review Interviews*. NY: Viking Press, 1984 (7th series).

192. **Joel Harnett** (1925–), American advertiser—fashion design

This city is the size of a country, but it has been operated like a candy store. (1976)

Note: Quotation from a speech delivered to the City Club of New York on May 7, 1976.
Source: Alec Lewis. *The Quotable Quotations*. NY: Thomas Crowell, 1980.

193. *Harper's Monthly* (1850–), American magazine, presently Harper's Magazine, published by Harper's Foundation

New York is notoriously the largest and least loved of any of our great cities . . . It is never the same city for a dozen years altogether. A man born in New York forty years ago finds nothing, absolutely nothing, of New York he knew. If he chances to stumble upon a few old houses not yet leveled, he is fortunate. (1856)

Source: Editorial of June 1856.

194. **Michael Harrington** (1928–), American author, social issues

The looseness, the brashness, the rhythm of Harlem give it a life of its own. . . . If you take a walk in Harlem, if you look behind the charming stereotype you will find two things involved in one way or another in every gesture and every word spoken in the ghetto. The double indignity of racial discrimination and economic oppression. . . . (1960s)

Source: Michael Harrington. *Poverty in the United States*. NY: Macmillan, 1962.

◆ ◆ ◆

New York was the only city in the United States that did not need a booster organization. . . . [W]e simply assumed that we were the best—in baseball as well as intellect, in brashness and in subtlety, in everything—and it would have been unseemly to remark upon such an obvious fact. (1973)

Source: Michael Harrington. *Fragments of the Century*. NY: Saturday Review Press/Dutton, 1973.

195. **Bill Harris** (1933–   ), American author, history topics

People . . . in the other twelve colonies viewed New Yorkers with almost the same animosity they felt for Londoners . . . they were convinced that New York was the most sin ridden city of the North American continent. There were brothels in the City of Brotherly Love, and it was estimated that there was a tavern in every eighth building in Boston, but New York had more of both than either city. Americans from the Carolinas and Maine continually castigated the New Yorkers for not being "church people." (1989)

Note: Description of New York City shortly before the 1776 Revolution.
Source: Bill Harris. *The History of New York City*. NY: Archive Publishing, 1989.

196. **Sydney J. Harris** (1917–   ), American author

The lusts of the flesh can be gratified anywhere; it is not this sort of license that distinguishes New York. It is rather, a lust of the total ego for recognition, even for eminence. More than elsewhere, everybody here wants to be Somebody. (1953)

Source: Sydney J. Harris. *Strictly Personal*. Chicago, IL: Regnery Co., 1953.

197. **James A. Harrison** (1848–1911), American author, editor and literary critic

New York literature may be taken as a fair representation of that of the country at large. The city itself is the focus of American letters. Its authors include, perhaps, one fourth of all in America, and the influence they exert on their brethren, if seemingly silent, is not the less extensive and decisive. (1903)

Source: James Harrison. *The Complete Works of Edgar Allan Poe,* Vol. 15 (Introduction). NY: AMS Press, 1965 (reprint of 1902 edition).

198. **Wallace K. Harrison** (1895–1981), Chief architect of the United Nations Building in New York City

When we started the UN we were not trying to make a monument. We were building a workshop—a workshop for world peace. And we tried to make it the best damn workshop we could. (1952)

Note: The United Nations Building remains to this day a landmark attraction for both Americans and foreigners alike.
Source: *Time* (magazine), September 22, 1952

199. **Moss Hart** (1904–1961), American dramatist and librettist

The only credential the city asked was the boldness to dream. For those who did, it unlocked its gates and treasures, not caring who they were or where they came from. (1959)

◆　◆　◆

Poor people know poor people, rich people know rich people. It is one of the few things La Rochefoucault did not say, but then La Rochefoucault never lived in the Bronx. (1959)

Source: Moss Hart. *Act One*. NY: Random House, 1989.

200. **Nathaniel Hawthorne** (1804–1864), American novelist and short story writer

I intend to adhere to my former plan, of writing one or two mythological story books, to be published under O'Sullivan's auspices in New York—which is the only place where books can be published, with a chance of profit. (1843)

Note: Reference is made to an editor of the Democratic Review *in NYC.*
Source: Nathaniel Hawthorne. *The Letters, 1813–1843* (ed. by Thomas Woodson et al.). Cleveland, OH: Ohio State University Press, 1984.

201. **Helen Hayes** (1900–1993), American actress and author

The most positive thing of all is that nobody ever has to be alone in New York. You're alone with New York, which makes a whole world of difference. What other companion could be so varied, stimulating, dramatic and so available? (1972)

◆　◆　◆

The [Greenwich] Village still has the most varied population in New York. It is the one place where you can meet anybody: Puerto Ricans, Italians, Blacks, hippies, middle-class whites, and just bums. Why is it that these people normally at each other's throats have peaceably accepted polychrome integration is the most fascinating thing about the Village. (1972)

Source: Helen Hayes and Anita Loos. *Twice Over Lightly: New York Then and Now*. NY: Harcourt, Brace, Jovanovich, 1972.

202. **Joel Tyler Headley** (1813–1897), American historian and author

At the average rate of two every week, one hanged and one

burned alive, they [black people] were hurried into eternity amid prayers, and imprecation, and shrieks of agony. The hauling of the wood to the stake, and the preparation of the gallows, kept the inhabitants in a state of bordering on insanity. (1873)

Note: Description of reprisals of Black riots during 1712–1741 in New York City.
Source: Joel Tyler Headley. *The Great Riots of New York, 1712–1773.* NY: E. B. Treat, 1873.

203. **Lafcadio Hearn** (1850–1904), Author, literary critic, and translator, born Yakumo Koizumi (of Irish and Greek parents)

The city [NYC] drives me crazy, if you prefer, crazier; and I have no peace of mind or rest of body till I get out of it. Nobody can find any body, nothing seems to be anywhere, everything seems to be mathematics and geometry and enigmatics and riddles and confusion worse confounded: architecture and mechanics run mad. . . . I think an earthquake might produce some improvements. (1889)

Source: Lafcadio Hearn. *Life and Letters of Lafcadio Harn* (ed. by Elisabeth Bisland). Boston: Houghton Mifflin, 1906.

204. **Ben Hecht** (1894–1964), American columnist, dramatist, and novelist

A city where wise guys peddle gold bricks to each other and Truth, crushed down to earth, rises again as phoney as a glass eye. (1922)

Source: Ben Hecht. *Gaily, Gaily.* Chicago, IL: Covici-McGee, 1922.

205. **Joseph Heller** (1923–   ), American novelist

That part of New York that we think of as hospitable has

grown smaller and smaller and now includes maybe four or five neighborhoods. . . . It's still a place you get very quick answers, though it may be a rude answer. (1994)

Source: *Spirit* (Southwestern Airlines). October 1994.

206. **Ernest Hemingway** (1899–1961), American author and journalist

[L]iterary New York [is] a bottle full of tapeworms trying to feed on each other. (1950s)

Source: John Updike. *Picked Up Pieces*. NY: Alfred Knopf, 1976

207. **William H. Hemp** (NDA), American author and illustrator

Overshadowed by skyscrapers, wedged between warehouses, hidden behind creaky iron gates, and tucked away like treasure chests in pirate caves, you find the enclaves of New York: the alleys, the cul-de-sacs, quiet courts, colorful market places, nostalgic neighborhoods, secluded squares, and story book streets that make up the mosaic of Manhattan Island today. (1975)

Source: William H. Hemp. *New York Enclaves*. NY: Clarkson N. Potter, 1975.

208. **O. Henry** (1862–1910), American short story writer, born William Sydney Porter

Humanity was gone from them [New Yorkers]; they were toddling idols of stone and varnish, worshiping themselves and greedy. . . . Frozen, cruel, implacable, impervious, cut to an identical pattern, they hurried on their ways like statues brought by some miracles to motion, while soul and feeling lay unroused in the reluctant marble. (1907)

Source: *Short Stories of America*. Boston: Houghton Mifflin, 1921.

◆ ◆ ◆

[E]very man jack when he first sets foot on the stones of Manhattan has got to fight. He has got to fight at once until either he or his adversary wins. There is no resting between rounds. . . . It is a fight to a finish (1908)

Source: Melusina Fay Peirce. *New York: A Symphonic Study.* NY: Neale Publishing, 1908.

209. **Bob Herbert** (1929–   ), American journalist, NYT columnist

If you are a New Yorker the fear is there, somewhere, maybe buried deep beneath the surface of consciousness, or maybe right out there in the open. . . . [T]he fear is that from out of the chaos some maniac will emerge to pointlessly, stupidly, inexplicably hurl you, blast you, cast you into oblivion. (1995)

Note: Quote refers to several killings of New Yorkers by mentally ill people in recent years.
Source: *New York Times.* January 7, 1995.

210. **Don Herold** (1889–1966), American author and artist

There is nothing distinctive about living in New York; over eight million other people are doing it. (1960s)

Source: Herbert V. Prochnow. *The Toastmaster's Treasure Chest.* NY: Harper & Row, 1988.

211. **Harry Hershfield** (1885–1974), American author and illustrator

New York is a city where everyone mutinies but no one deserts. (1965)

Source: *New York Times.* December 5, 1965.

212. **Al Hirschfield** (1903–   ), American cartoonist and illustrator

There was a log-rolling period when everyone was considered a genius and praised each other's work, like the Round Table. Now, it's as if everyone is husbanding a secret, a gimmick they don't want to share with other people. It's become all clickey. (1995)

Note: Quotation compares the atmosphere of the literati circle at the Algonquin Hotel's Round Table in New York of the 1930s to the present atmosphere among artists.
Source: *New York Times,* December 14, 1995.

213. **Edward Hoaglund** (1932–   ), American author and essayist

We New Yorkers see more death and violence than most soldiers do, grow a thick chitin on our backs, grimace like a rat and learn to do a disappearing act. Long ago we outgrew the need to be blowhards about our masculinity. (1988)

Source: Edward Hoagland. *The Best of Edward Hoagland: Essays from Twenty Years.* NY: Summit Books, 1988.

214. **Simon Hoggart** (1946–   ), British journalist and author

Living in New York is like being at some terrible late-night party. You're tired, you've had a headache since you arrived, but you can't leave because then you'd miss the party. (1990)

Source: Simon Hoggart. *America: A User's Guide.* NY: Fontana/ Harper Collins, 1991.

215. **Oliver Wendell Holmes** (1809–1894), American physician, author, and poet

I have seen next to nothing *grandiose,* out of New York, in all our cities. It makes 'em all look paltry and petty. Has many elements of civilization. May stop where Venice did, though, for aught we know . . . all that did not make Venice the brain of Italy. (1860)

Source: Oliver Wendell Holmes. *The Professor at the Breakfast Table: With the Story of Iris.* Boston: Ticknor & Fields, 1860.

216. **Philip Hone** (1780–1851), American businessman, author, and NYC mayor

The gambling in stocks in Wall Street has arrived at such a pitch, and the sudden reverses of fortunes are so frequent that it is a matter of everyday intelligence that some unlucky rascal has lost other people's money to a large amount and run away, or been caught and consigned to the hand of justice. . . . [B]ut the chasm on the face of society which his detection and removal occasions is filled up in a day or two. . . . [T]he catastrophe of Monday is forgotten by Saturday night. (1835)

◆ ◆ ◆

Our good city of New York has already arrived at the state of society to be found in large cities of Europe: overburdened with population, and where the two extremes of costly luxury in living, expensive establishments, and improvident waste are presented in daily and hourly contrast with squalid misery and hopeless destitution. This state of things has been hastened by the constant stream of European paupers arriving upon the shores of this land of promise. (1847)

Source: Philip Hone. *The Diary of Philip Hone, 1828–1851* (ed. by Allan Nevins). NY: Dodd, Mead, 1936.

217. **Irving Howe** (1920–   ), American Jewish author, editor, translator

[Lower East Side] . . . soon came to form the social, economic and intellectual center of the Yiddish speaking world in America. Here were the main writers; the best theaters; here, the leading intellectuals; here, the headquarters of the Jewish parties and organizations, but here, above all, during the early decades of this century, a tightly packed mass of immigrants who, in part because of their sheer density of numbers, brought to fruition the culture of Yiddish. (1979)

Note: Description refers to the Lower East Side in the 19th century.
Source: Irving Howe and Kenneth Libo. *How We Lived: A Documentary History of Immigrant Jews in America.* NY: Richard Marek Publisher, 1979.

218. **William Dean Howells** (1837–1920), American editor, author, and critic

I look forward to a winter in New York with loathing, I would so much rather be in the country; but it will be well for the work I am trying to do, and it seems the only thing for the children. Between the two cities [Boston and New York] I prefer New York; It is less done and there is more for one to see and learn there. (1891)

Note: From a letter addressed to his father
Source: Edwin H. Cady. *The Realist War: The Mature Years, 1885–1920, of William Dean Howells.* Syracuse, NY: Syracuse University Press, 1958.

219. **Charles Hoyt** (1860–1900), American dramatist and poet

The Bowery (song)
The Bow'ry, the Bow'ry!
They say such things, and they do strange things
On the Bow'ry, the Bow'ry!
I'll never go there any more! (1891)

Note: Music by American composer Percy Gaunt (NDA)
Source: Ronny Schiff, ed. *America's Story in Songs.* NY: Warner
Brothers, 1975.

220. **Henry Hudson** (NDA–1611), English navigator, discovered the Hudson River

When I came on shore [in NYC Bay], the swarthy natives all
stood around and sung in their fashion; their clothing consisted of the skins of foxes and other animals, which they
dress and make the skins into garments of various sorts.
Their food is Turkish wheat [maize or Indian corn], whey
they cook by baking, and it is excellent eating. (1609)

*Note: Excerpt from author's diary; he initially landed on Coney
Island and proceeded to NY harbor as master of the ship* Half
Moon.
Source: Donald S. Johnson. *Charting the Sea of Darkness: The
Voyages of Henry Hudson.* Camden, ME: International Marine,
1993.

221. **Charles Evans Hughes** (1862–1948), American Secretary
of State, and Supreme Court Justice (1930–1941)

Any part of New York that had a bad reputation was particularly interesting. I wandered about Chatham Street, the
Five Points, Cherry Hills and various places that were notorious. The Bowery was a fascinating place and little escaped my curious eye. . . . [T]he stretches of the lower East
Side, then predominantly Irish, became very familiar.
(1874)

*Note: The author was only twelve years old when he made his first
trip to New York and recorded this thought.*
Source: Betty Glad. *Charles Evans Hughes and the Illusions of Innocence: A Study in American Diplomacy.* Urbana, IL: University of Illinois Press, 1966.

222. **Langston Hughes** (1902–1967), African American author

Harlem, like a Picasso painting in his cubistic period. Harlem—Southern Harlem—the Carolinas, Georgia, Florida—
looking for the promised land—dressed in rhythmic words,
painted in bright pictures, dancing jazz—and ending up
in the subway at morning rushtime—*headed downtown.*
(1925)

Source: *Freedomways* (magazine). Summer 1963.

◆ ◆ ◆

Melting pot Harlem—Harlem of honey and chocolate and
caramel and rum and vinegar and lemon and lime and gall . . .
where the subway from the Bronx keeps right downtown. (1963)

Source: John Henrik Clarke. *Harlem, USA.* NY: Collier Books,
1971 (revised edition).

223. **James Gibbons Huneker** (1860–1921), American art critic

[NYC is] a vast cauldron [where] every race bubbles and
boils and fuses in the dear old dirty, often disreputable,
though never dull East Side. (1915)

Source: James Huneker. *New Cosmopolis.* NY: C. Scribner's
Sons, 1915.

224. **Ada Louise Huxtable** (1921?–), American architecture
critic, historian, and consultant

In New York, neighborhoods fall like dominoes. Everyone
knows about the small electrical supply stores uprooted by
the World Trade Center; the thrift and antique shops chased
by the apartment builders from Third Avenue; the small
businesses, bars and coffee dealers displaced from the
Lower Manhattan waterfront by office construction; the

artists lofts, eliminated in the [Greenwich] Village for more luxury apartments. (1970)

Source: Ada Louise Huxtable. *Will They Finish Bruckner Boulevard?* NY: Macmillan, 1970.

225. **Ivo Indjev** (1955–   ), Bulgarian journalist and editor

Oh, oh, I'm an alien in New York—this song of Sting's came into my mind the very moment I realized that I am going to the [United] States. However, the text did not apply to me. I just did not feel like an alien in New York. It was my first time in the States and I was not especially impressed. . . . I would have been more impressed if the image I had of America had proven exaggerated. (1994)

Source: *Eurasian Press Monitor.* Vol. I, December 1994/January 1995.

226. **William Inge** (1913–1973), American playwright and author

It wasn't until I got to New York that I became Kansan. Everyone kept reminding me that they were Jewish or Irish, or whatever, so I kept reminding them that I was Middle-western. Before I knew it, I actually began to brag about being from Kansas! I discovered that I had something unique, but it was the nature of New York that forced me to claim my past. (1941)

Source: Joseph McCrindle. *Behind the Scenes: Theater and Film Interviews from the Transatlantic Review.* NY: Holt, Rinehart, Winston, 1971.

227. **Nicolae Iorga** (1871–1940), Romanian historian and author

The Statue of Liberty. She certainly impresses. Arisen from the mist in front of the great human wave, she stands straight and orders with the imperative of a gesture of salvation. Regardless of the opinions about its value, and criticisms on account of its proportions, she possesses the advantage of proclaiming a moral concept, one of the most seducing and noble ideas . . . able to mobilize energies from all corners of the world. (1930)

Source: Nicolae Iorga. *America and the Romanians from America: Voyage Notes and Conferences.* Valenii de Munte, Romania: Datina Romaneasca, 1930 (title and the quotation translated from the Romanian).

228. **Washington Irving** (1783–1859), American novelist, essayist, and historian

The renowned and ancient city of Gotham. (1807)

Note: It is believed that this was the earliest reference to NYC, probably inspired from Gotham, England, inhabited by people doing strange things
Source: Washington Irving. *Salmagundi; or the Whim-Whams and Opinions of Lancelot Langstaff.* NY: Longworth, 1807–1808.

229. **Jesse Jackson** (1941–   ), African American clergyman, civil rights leader

Take New York, the dynamic metropolis. What makes New York so special? It's the invitation of the Statue of Liberty—give me your tired, your poor, your huddled masses who yearn to breathe free. Not restricted to English only. (1988)

Source: *New York Times.* July 20, 1988.

230. **Kenneth A. Jackson** (1939–   ), American university professor and editor of *Encyclopedia of New York City*

The thing I've found is the people that are most enthusiastic about living in New York are often people like me who are originally from somewhere else . . . New Yorkers are more jaded. They take it for granted . . . It's the newcomers that have tried the other—that have experienced the grass, and the narrowness of most American life—and find something extraordinarily liberating about New York. (1995)

Source: *Manhattan Spirit,* November 9, 1995 (a Manhattan weekly paper.

231. **Phil Jackson** (1945–   ), American basketball player

One of the things that amaze me is the energy that's in New York. You get no energy from the earth because the earth is all covered up with cement and bricks. There's no place to walk on earth unless you go to Central Park. The energy all comes from human beings. (1976)

Source: Bill Bradley. *Life on the Run.* NY: Quadrangle/New York Times Book Co., 1976.

232. **Henry James** (1843–1916), American (NYC-born) short-story writer and novelist

It is altogether an extraordinary growing, swarming, glittering, pushing, chattering, good-natured, cosmopolitan place, and perhaps in some ways the best imitation of Paris that can be found (yet with a great originality of its own). (1883)

Source: Henry James. *Letters* (4 volumes). Cambridge, MA: Belknap/Harvard University Press, 1984.

◆ ◆ ◆

The ambiguity is the element in which the whole thing swims for me—so nocturnal, so bacchanal, so hugely hatted and feathered and flounded, yet apparently so innocent, almost so patriarchal again, and matching, in its mixture, with nothing one had elsewhere known. It breathed its simple

"New York! New York!" at every impulse of inquiry; so that I can only echo contentedly, with analysis for once quite agreeably baffled, remarkable, unspeakable New York. (1907)

Source: Henry James. *The American Scene*. NY: Horizon Press, 1967 (reprint of 1907 edition).

233. **Rian James** (1899–NDA), American author and screen playwright

New York is impatient of its past; jealous of its present, and totally unconcerned as to its future. . . . New York is the greatest, grandest, most glorious show on earth—and it's never closed. It's more than a city—it's an adventure compressed within thirty one pulsating miles. (1931)

◆ ◆ ◆

[Greenwich Village] is lotus land in which gaiety is synthetic, poverty is fashionable and real, hilarity is forced, honor is infrequent, purpose is pie eyed, ambition is asleep, and art is merely an excuse for everything. (1931)

Source: Rian James. *All About New York*. NY: John Day, 1931.

234. **Theodore James Jr.** (1934–   ), American journalist

The Empire State Building is more than just another very tall manmade structure. . . . Despite the very grand schemes for other buildings, it is undoubtedly certain that none will ever match its flawless lines or rival its startling beauty. And in the final analysis, none can ever capture the imagination of the entire world as has the Empire State Building. (1975)

Source: Theodore James Jr. *The Empire State Building*. NY: Harper & Row, 1975.

235. **Thomas Alibone Janvier** (1846–1913), American historian and author

The flag of the Dutch West India Company fell from Fort Amsterdam, and the flag of England went up over what then became Fort James. Governor Stuyvesant—even his wooden leg sharing in his air of dejection—marched dismally his conquered forces out from the main gateway . . . at the same time the English marched gallantly down Broadway . . . and Governor Nichols solemnly took possession of New Amsterdam, and of New Netherland in the name of the English sovereign, and for the use of Duke of York. (1894)

Note: This event took place on September 8, 1664.
Source: Thomas A. Janvier. *In Old New York.* NY: Harper & Brothers, 1922 (reprint of 1894 ed.).

236. **Oliver O. Jensen** (1914–   ), American author

Is New York a den of vice? When a bishop later proclaims that there are as many prostitutes in New York as there are Methodists, the city administration sniggers. (1969)

Source: *American Heritage* (magazine). December 1969.

237. **Father Isaac Jogues** (1607–1646), French Catholic missionary among the American Indians

On the Island of Manhatte, and its environs, there may well be four or five hundred men of different sects and nations. The Director General told me that there were men of eighteen different languages. They are scattered here on the river, as the beauty and convenience of the spot invited each to settle. (1643)

Note: At that time the name of the island was Manhatte, *the original Indian American name*

Source: Felix Martin. *The Life of Father Isaac Jogues.* NY: Benziger Brothers, 1885.

238. **James Weldon Johnson** (1871–1938), African American poet and educator

My City (poem)
But, ah! Manhattan's sights and sounds, her smells
Her crowds, her throbbing force, the thrill that comes
From being of her a part, her subtle spells, her slums—
Oh God! the stark unutterable pity,
To be dead, and never again behold my city! (1922)

Source: James Weldon Johnson. *Black Manhattan.* NY: Arno Press, 1968 (reprint of 1930 ed.).

♦ ♦ ♦

In the history of New York the name Harlem has changed from Dutch to Irish to Jewish to Negro. But it is through this last change that it gained the most widespread fame throughout coloured America. Harlem is the recognized Negro capital. Indeed, it is the Mecca for the sightseer, the pleasure-seeker, the curious, the adventurous, the enterprising, the ambitious, and the talented of the entire Negro world . . . (1930)

Source: James Weldon Johnson. *Black Manhattan.* Salem, NH: Ayer Company, 1988 (reprint of 1930 edition).

239. **Shirley Jones** (1934–   ), American, Academy Award-winning actress

When I first met my Brooklyn knight-in-armor, I fell like a ton of Flatbush bricks. And while the world sent me smelling verts and books on "miss-mating", I sometimes felt differently . . . The cracking glint in the man's eye and the unending stream of raspy pronouncements absolutely bewitched me. (1995)

Note: Description of first impressions about Brooklyn-born future husband (Marty Ingels); Flatbush is a neighborhood in Brooklyn.
Source: *Modern Maturity,* November–December 1995.

240. **Erica Jong** (1942–   ), American author and poet

[T]here are . . . things in New York that are very distracting. Too many parties. Too many telephone calls. Too many people. Yet when I found myself last summer at Cape Cod sitting alone—for hours—and listening to the ocean, trees and stuff, I would call long distance New York because it was too quiet. (1974)

Source: William Packard, ed. *The Craft of Poetry: Interviews from the New York Quarterly.* NY: Doubleday, 1974.

241. **Robert Juet (de Lime-House)** (NDA–1611), one of Henry Hudson's crew members, later demoted because of mutiny

We anchored in a bay [NYC] on the other side of the river. . . . [H]ere there was a good piece of ground and a cliff close by of white-green color. . . . [I]t is on the river called MANNA-HATA no people there came to trouble us and we rode quietly all night. (1609)

Source: Donald S. Johnson. *Charting the Sea of Darkness: The Voyages of Henry Hudson.* Camden, ME: International Marine, 1993.

242. **Roger Kahn** (1927–   ), American author

Brooklyn had been a heterogenous, dominantly middle-class community, with remarkable schools, good libraries, and not only major league baseball, but extensive concert series, second-run movie houses, expensive neighborhoods and a lovely rolling stretch of acreage called Prospect Park. For all the outsiders' jokes, middle-brow Brooklyn was reasonably sure of its cosmic place, and safe. (1945)

Source: Roger Kahn. *The Boys of Summer*. NY: Harper & Row, 1972.

243. **Peter Kalm** (1716–1779), Swedish naturalist and traveler

New York probably carries on a more extensive commerce than any town in English North American provinces; at least it may be said to equal them: Boston and Philadelphia however, come very near up to it. The trade of New York extends to many places; as it is said they send more ships from thence to London, than they do from Philadelphia. (1748)

Source: Peter Kalm. *Travels into North America* (translated from Swedish by John Reinhold Forester). Barre, MA: Imprint Society, 1972.

244. **Donna Karan** (1948–   ), American fashion designer

The best thing about New York is that every place you go is like a little world. There are all these little . . . mini-worlds. If you want a taste of Italy, it's there. There is a little piece of the world in every corner. (1993)

Source: *New York* (magazine). December 20–27, 1993.

245. **Danny Kaye** (1913–1987), American theater and television actor, born David Daniel Kaminsky

I think I benefited by being born and raised in Brooklyn. That was one of the most cosmopolitan neighborhoods . . . — it's where I learned you didn't dislike anybody because he was an Italian, a Jew, an Irishman or what else. There were great cultural differences but you stood on your merit as a youngster. (1971)

Source: *New York Times*. February 21, 1971.

246. **Alfred Kazin** (1915–   ), American author, essayist, and literary critic

No other city for the greater part of the century has been so immediately recognizable for corporate drive, technical daring and flair, the composition of thrusting, uprearing masses of buildings, one group rising on the wave created by the other and still another. New York created skyline as the proof that any city in the world, no matter what else surrounds it, can be modern. (1989)

Source: Alfred Kazin and David Finn (photos). *Our New York.* NY: Harper & Row, 1989.

◆ ◆ ◆

I was excited . . . by the whirl of New York and the high lean towers of Radio City [Music Hall], excited even more by the women in the morning light, the breasts and the hot purple mouth of the Bergdorf [Goodman] women, the fantastic sexiness of New York at lunch in certain cool restaurants—all of it hot and cold at once, frightening to dream about. (1940)

Note: Kazin refers to New York in the 1940s. Bergdorf Goodman is an exclusive clothing store on 57th Street in NYC.
Source: *New Yorker* (magazine). March 7, 1994.

247. **Helen Keller** (1880–1968), American deaf and blind author and lecturer

Cut off as I am, it is inevitable that I should sometimes feel like a shadow walking in a shadowy world. When this happens

I ask to be taken to New York City. Always I return home weary but I have the comforting certainty that mankind is real and I myself am not a dream. (1929)

Source: Helen Keller. *Midstream: My Later Life* (ed. by Alexander Klein). NY: Greenwood Press, 1968.

248. **Gene Kelly** (1917–1996), American dancer and actor

New York has a marvelously strange physical effect on me. In Manhattan I walk faster than I do anywhere in the world because I am more exhilarated there than anywhere else. (1985)

Source: Roxie Munro. *Color New York*. NY: Timbre/Arbor House, 1985.

249. **Murray Kempton** (1917–   ), American author

The faces of New York remind me of people who played a game and lost. . . . A neighborhood is where, when you go out of it, you get beat up. (1963)

Source: Murray Kempton. *America Comes of Middle Age*. Boston: Little Brown, 1963.

250. **Jack Kerouac** (1922–1969), American author

Whenever spring comes to New York I can't stand the suggestions of the land that come blowing over the river from New Jersey and I've got to go. So I went. (1955)

Source: Jack Kerouac. *On the Road*. NY: Viking Press, 1957.

251. **Odette Keun** (1899–NDA), French travel author

You cannot realize, on Broadway, that you are in America. This is the rendezvous of an international POPULO, especially on a Saturday evening. . . . At every moment I meet nose to nose a racial type that comes from my own continent, or Africa, or Asia. The language you overhear isn't English either: Irish, German, Russian, Italian, Greek, Scandinavian, Jewish, all the accents, rolling, slurring, gargling, high-pitched, guttural, clipped, mangle and murder the Anglo-Saxon idiom. . . . (1939)

Source: Odette Keun. *I Think Aloud in America*. NY: Longman, Green, 1939.

252. **Dorothy Kilgallen** (1913–1965), American author

The world is grand, awfully big and astonishingly beautiful, frequently thrilling. But I love New York. (1936)

Source: Dorothy Kilgallen. *Girl Around the World*. Philadelphia: David McKay, 1936.

253. **Larry King** (1933–   ), Brooklyn-born (Zeiger) American TV personality, with own show on CNN

The beautiful thing about my years in Brooklyn was that it didn't take hindsight to appreciate it. We knew it was a great life while we were living it. Every day meant encounter with good people, shared experiences with glowing optimism of the future . . . we had friends and a sense of neighborhood and solid families and values. (1992)

Source: Larry King. *When You're from Brooklyn, Everything Else Is Tokyo*. Boston: Little, Brown, 1992.

254. **Eugene Kinkead** (1906–   ), American author, environmental issues

The Central Park, a national as well as a New York City treasure, is the most famous park in the United States and one of the most famous in the world . . . In the verdant world of the growing season, the Park becomes a shimmering green jewel in the forehead of Manhattan. With the burst of vegetation in the spring, the resurrection of the whole vegetable race occurs almost miraculously amid the surrounding lifeless brick and stone. (1990)

Source: Eugene Kinkead. *Central Park, 1857–1995: The Birth, Decline and Renewal of a National Treasure.* NY: W. W. Norton, 1990.

255. **Gwen Kinkead** (1951–   ), American author and journalist

At the Southern end of Manhattan is the largest Chinese community in the Western hemisphere. The crooked streets of one of New York's oldest ghettos smell of salt and fish and orange peel. This booming, chaotic, little piece of China overflowing with new immigrants, is a remarkably self-contained neighborhood — virtually a nation unto itself. To a degree almost impossible to outsiders to comprehend, most of its inhabitants lead lives segregated from the rest of America. (1992).

Source: Gwen Kinkead. *Chinatown: A Portrait of a Closed Society.* NY: Harper Collins, 1992.

256. **Lord John Kinross** (1904–1976), British author and biographer

But the classic view of New York skyline — this time downtown skyline of Wall Street — is from the Brooklyn waterfront. Here, on my third evening in New York, I look across the river . . . to see range upon range of towers, racing upwards to a chaotic variety of heights, yet so compressed as to make an orderly form out of chaos. (1960)

◆ ◆ ◆

New York is a quiet sort of place, where nobody much

knows anybody else, and the people work hard or pretend to, and go to bed with a glass of milk, having previously hotted up a hamburger in an immaculate five thousand dollar kitchen. (1960)

Source: John Kinross. *The Innocents at Home*. NY: Morrow, 1960.

257. **Rudyard Kipling** (1865–1936), British writer and poet

It is not easy to escape from a big city. An entire continent was waiting to be travelled, and for that reason, we lingered in New York till the city felt so homelike that it seemed wrong to leave it. And further, the more one studied it, the more grotesque bad it grew—bad in its paving, bad in its streets, bad in its street-police, and but for the kindness of the tides, would be worse than bad in its sanitary arrangements. (1892)

Source: Rudyard Kipling. *Letters of Travel, 1892–1913*. Garden City, NY: Doubleday, Page & Co, 1920.

258. **Andrei Klenov** (1920–   ), Russian American author

To remain indifferent to New York is not possible—you can fall in love with this city and remain fond of it forever, or you can bestow upon it your negative feelings and easily curse it: dirty, neglected, disgusting subway; South Bronx and other neighborhoods resemble Stalingrad during and after the battle [WWII]. . . . New York can also be called the "city Mammon" as [Maxim] Gorky did, but New York can also be glorified as the city of the future. . . . (1983)

Source: Andrei Klenov. *Pictures of New York (Kartinki N'iu Iorka)*. NY: Parus, 1983 (title and quotation translated from the Russian).

259. **Fletcher Knebel** (1911–), American author

No other city in the United States can divest the visitor of so much money with so little enthusiasm. In Dallas, they take away with gusto; in New Orleans, with a bow; in San Francisco, with a wink and a grin. In New York, you're lucky if you get a grunt. (1963)

Source: *Look* (magazine). March 26, 1963.

260. **Henry Knox** (1750–1806), American Revolutionary General

New York is a place where I think in general the houses are better built than in Boston. They are generally of brick and three stories high with the largest kind of windows. Their churches are grand; their college, work-house, and the hospitals most excellently situated and also exceedingly commodious, their principal streets much wider than ours. (1776)

◆ ◆ ◆

The people [of NYC] . . . are magnificent: in their equipages which are numerous, in their house furniture which is fine, in their pride and conceit which are inimitable, in their profaneness which is intolerable, in the want of principle which is prevalent, in their Toryism which is insufferable, and for which they must repent in dust and ashes. (1776)

Source: George Scheer. *Rebels and Redcoats*. Cleveland, OH: World Publishers, 1957.

261. **Edward Koch** (1924–), American lawyer, New York City Mayor from 1978–1989, and former U.S. Congressman

My own feeling is that I am an ordinary guy, with special abilities. But I want the things the average person wants. And so I do the things the average New Yorker would do if he or she were the mayor. (1983)

Source: Chris McNickle. *To Be Mayor of New York: Ethnic Politics in the City*. NY: Columbia University Press, 1993.

◆　◆　◆

Water, water everywhere
Atlantic and Pacific
But New York City's got them beat
Our aqua is terrific! (1984)

Note: Reference is made to the quality of water in NYC during a Convention of the American Water Works Association
Source: *New York Times*. June 11, 1984.

262. **Rem Koolhaas** (1944–   ), Dutch architect and author

Manhattan is the twentieth century Rosetta Stone. Not only are large parts of its surface occupied by architectural mutations (Central Park, the Skyscraper), utopian fragments (Rockefeller Center, the UN Building), and irrational phenomena (Radio City Music Hall), but in addition each block is covered with several layers of phantom architecture in the form of past occupancies, aborted projects and popular fantasies that provide alternative images to New York that exists. (1978)

Source: Rem Koolhaas. *Delirious New York: A Retroactive Manifesto for Manhattan*. NY: Oxford University Press, 1978.

263. **Mark Kramer** (1944–   ), American journalist and author

A veritable street fair of high risk behavior engulfs the neighborhood known as Rose Hill [Manhattan] each night from 12:30 A.M. until sunrise, when strolling prostitutes, their pimps and endless stream of sex-seeking males all embark on their illicit erotic agendas. An aura of danger and suspicion hangs heavy upon these off-off-peak traffic jams as hookers wobble from car to car on spike heels, proffering their charms to the drive-by carnal consumers within. (1994)

Source: *Our Town* (New York publication). June 30, 1994.

264. **Carol Herselle Krinsky** (1937–), American author and historian

The essence of New York . . . is its drive towards the future, its constant experimentation, its attempts to make the best of its physical limitations. . . . Visitors regard it [NYC] as the embodiment of material progress, of twentieth-century forces of physical size, of speed, of compromise, of ambition. There is no better representative of these forces than Rockefeller Center which established its neighborhood as the heart of New York City. (1978)

Source: Carol H. Krinsky. *Rockefeller Center*. NY: Oxford University Press, 1978.

265. **Louis Kronenberger** (1904–), American author, editor, and literary critic

It is one of the sublime provincialities of New York that its inhabitants lap up trivial gossip about essential nobodies they've never set eyes on, while continuing to boast that they could live somewhere for twenty years without so much as exchanging pleasantries with their neighbors across the hall. (1959)

Source: Louis Kronenberger. *Company Manners: A Cultural Inquiry into American Life*. Indianapolis, IN: Bobbs-Merrill, 1959.

266. **Alksandr Kwasniewski** (1954–), Poland's current president, elected in the country's 1995 general elections

To see blacks, whites, Indians, Orthodox Jews — it was unbelievable—people working together and having tolerance for each other. (1995)

Note: Impressions about New York City while Kwasniewski made a trip to USA in 1976.
Source: *New York Times,* November 29, 1995.

267. **Fiorello La Guardia** (1882–1947), American lawyer and politician, NYC Mayor from 1934 to 1945

My first qualification for this great office is my monumental personal ingratitude! (1934)

Note: Remark refers to the fact the La Guardia would not reward those who supported him in the elections with appointments to the city government.
Source: Ernest Cuneo. *Life with Fiorello: A Memoir.* NY: Macmillan, 1955.

268. **John Lambert** (175?–1823), British author and traveler

A public library is established at New York, which consists of about ten thousand volumes, many of them rare and valuable books. The building which contains them is situated in Nassau-Street. . . . There are also three or four public reading rooms and circulating libraries, which are supported by some of the principal booksellers, from the annual subscriptions of the inhabitants. There is a museum of natural curiosities in New York, but it contains nothing worthy of particular notice. . . . (1807)

Source: John Lambert. *Travels through Canada and the United States of North America in the Years 1806, 1807 and 1808.* London: C. Cradock and W. Joy, 1814.

269. **Abbot John Lardner** (1912–1960), American author

As a city, New York moves in the forefront of today's great

trend of great cities toward neurosis. She is confused, self-pitying, helpless and dependent. (1953)

Source: *New York Times*. February 1, 1953.

270. **D. H. (David Herbert) Lawrence** (1885–1930), British novelist and poet

New York looks as ever: stiff, machine-made, and against nature. It is so mechanical there is not the sense of death. (1924)

Source: Peter Yap, ed. *Traveller's Dictionary of Quotations: Who Said What, About Where*. London/Boston: Routledge & Kegan Paul, 1983.

271. **Emma Lazarus** (1849–1887), American poet

The Statue of Liberty (poem)
Give me your tired, your poor,
Your huddled masses yearning to breathe free
The wretched refuse of your teeming shore,
Send these, the homeless, tempest tossed to me,
I lift my lamp beside the golden door. (1883)

Source: Emma Lazarus. *The Poems of Emma Lazarus* (2 vols.) Boston: Houghton Mifflin, 1889.

272. **Adrian Nicole Le Blank** (1952–   ), Fellow of Bunting Institute at Radcliffe

Gang life remains the best version of girlhood [at Brooklyn Navy Yard] . . . a way to hang out with the movable boys as more than a girlfriend, to get comfort and protection and a public code to live by. . . . It distances from other under-girls-school girls in "lock down" by panicked parents, teenage mothers in lock down by obsessive husbands, girls who are battered, youth counselors who are themselves battered, women and girls . . . under the thumbs of less violent men. (1994)

Source: *New York Times Magazine.* August 14, 1994.

273. **Fran Lebowitz** (1951?–   ), American humorist and author

[I]t [Soho] was positively awash in hardwood floors, talked-to plants, indoor swings, enormous record collections, hiking boots, conceptual artists, video communes, Art book stores, Art grocery stores, Art restaurants, Art bars, Art galleries, and boutiques selling tie-dyed raincoats, macrame flower pots, and Art Deco salad plates. (1978)

Source: Fran Lebowitz. *Metropolitan Life.* NY: Henry Robbins Books/E. P. Dutton, 1978.

274. **Le Corbusier** (1887–1965), French, Swiss-born architect, painter, and author, originally named Charles Edouard Jeanneret-Gris

A hundred times have I thought New York is a catastrophe . . . it is a beautiful catastrophe. (1961)

Source: *New York Herald Tribune.* August 6, 1961.

◆ ◆ ◆

It [the RCA Building] is rational, logically conceived, biologically normal, harmonious in its four functional elements: halls—for the entrance and division of crowds, grouped shafts for vertical circulation (elevators), corridors (internal streets), regular offices. (1964)

Source: Le Corbusier. *When the Cathedrals Were White* (transl. from the French by Frank Huslod). NY: McGraw-Hill, 1964.

275 **Gary Lee** (1956–   ), American journalist

For African Americans, no community in the country is more pregnant with cultural reference and historical footnotes than these two square miles [Harlem] of brownstones and brick along the Northern end of the Island of Manhattan. This is the bohemia that poet Langston Hughes chronicled in rhyme, the painter William Johnson embellished in bright oils, and photographer James Vanderzee captured in daguerreotype-like portraits. . . . [T]his is earth that gave us the rose that Aretha Franklin told us to watch as she grows. . . . This is Harlem. (1994)

Source: *Washington Post.* October 30, 1994.

276. **Fernand Léger** (1882–1955), French painter

To create luxury with simplicity, that is the modern problem and Radio City [Music Hall] has solved it. (1935)

Source: *Art Front* (magazine). December 1935.

277. **Alan Lelchuck** (1938–   ), American novelist

For us in Brooklyn, there was the feeling that not only had we made it through—we were on the way up. We had a lot of motivation, we children of immigrants. There was a tremendous amount of talent pooled together to be the smartest, the best, the wittiest, the most mischievous. We had the desire to work hard plus the belief we could do anything. The myth of invincibility was very important. (1993)

Source: Myrna Frommer and Harvey Frommer. *It Happened in Brooklyn: An Oral History of Growing up in the Borough in the 1940s, 1950s, and 1960s.* NY: Harcourt Brace, 1993.

278. **John Lennon** (1940–1980), British rock musician

New York is what Paris was in the twenties . . . the center of
the art world. And we want to be in the center. It's the greatest place on earth. . . . I've got a lot of friends here and I even
brought my own cash. (1975)

Source: *The Tomorrow Show*. April 1975.

279. **William Ellery Leonard** (1876–1944), American poet and
author

New York in Sunset (poem)
The island city [Manhattan] of dominion stands
Crowned with all turrets, o'er water's crest,
Throned, like the bright Cybele of the West,
And hailed with cimbals in a million hands. (1914)

Source: Hamilton Fish Armstrong, ed. *The Book of New York's
Verse*. NY: G. P. Putnam's Sons, 1917.

280. **Sir Shane Leslie** (1885–1971), British author, editor, and
biographer

It [New York] was a frost-bitten city which I had not seen for
fifteen years. . . . But it was a different New York. It was like
Babel the morning after the building had to stop. And curi-
ously enough the same curse of languages had descended.
Every time the car stopped I heard a new tongue. New York
is not an American city. It is like an enormous waiting-room
in a railway depot fixed between the two hemispheres. (1934)

Source: Leslie Shane. *American Wonderland: Memoirs of Four
Tours in the United States of America, 1911–1935*. London: M.
Joseph, 1936.

281. **Philip Levin** (1928–), American author and poet

For years I loved the city, loved it so much I worked for

pittances just to live there and no matter how far it drove me into debt I felt it was worth it. (1950s)

Source: Philip Levin. *The Bread on Time: Toward an Autobiography.* NY: Alfred Knopf, 1994.

282. **Emory Lewis** (1919–   ), American author and editor

If the New Yorker has a fault, it is his arrogance or, in a milder form, supercilious manner toward those unfortunate enough not to be New Yorkers. . . . [H]e has cause for this intense chauvinism. New York does seem to have everything . . . but the New Yorker can be forgiven much, for he does live, after all, on the most fabulous island within the recorded history of man. (1963)

Source: Emory Lewis. *Cue's New York.* NY: Duell, Sloan and Pierce, 1963.

283. **A. Leyles** (1889–1966), American Yiddish-language poet and journalist, born Aron Glanz

New York (poem)
Metal. Granite. Uproar: racket clatter.
Automobile. Bus. Subway. El.
Burlesque. Grotesque. Cafe. Movie theater.
Electric light in screeching maze. A spell. (1956)

Source: Benjamin and Barbara Harshaw, eds. *American Yiddish Poetry: A Bilingual Anthology.* Berkeley: University of California Press, 1986.

284. **Janet Elaine Rubenson Lieberman** (1921–   ), American author

Every Sunday the place [North Beach, Queens] swarms with the lowest class of East Side toughs and girls young in years and old in vice. Nevertheless we see girls of respectable parents going there perhaps out of curiosity, and thereafter, caught by the whirl of excitement and crowds and music, each succeeding visit is but one step nearer moral ruin. The metropolitan policemen . . . are unanimous in saying that it is the worst place and the most toothsome crowd they ever encountered. (1905)

Note: Lieberman reproduced this paragraph from a local news-paper.

Source: Janet Lieberman and Richard Lieberman. *City Limits: A Social History of Queens.* Dubuque, IA: Kendall/Hunt Publishers, 1983.

285. *Life* (magazine) (1928–   ), American monthly published by Time-Life Company

Seventh Avenue working population is all caught up in the frenzied never-finished business of supplying new clothes for the American woman. The haughty Paris houses may often pioneer new styles, but it is the Seventh Avenue that translates them into wearable — and buyable — reality for the United States. (1960)

Note: New York's clothing industry and business is concentrated on Seventh Avenue, between Times Square and Twenty-Third Street.

Source: Editorial of October 3, 1960

286. **John Vliet Lindsay** (1921–   ), American politician and lawyer, NYC Mayor from 1966 to 1973

New York has total depth in every area. Washington has only politics; after that, the second thing is white marble. (1963)

Source: *Vogue* (magazine). August 1963.

♦   ♦   ♦

Not only is New York City the nation's melting pot, it is also the casserole, the chafing dish, and the charcoal grill. (1966)

Source: *New York Times*. November 10, 1966.

287. **N. Vachel Lindsay** (1879–1931), American poet

Rhyme about an Electrical Advertising Sign (poem)
Some day this Broadway shall climb to the skies.
As a ribbon of cloud on soul-wind shall rise
And we shall be lifted, rejoicing by night,
Till we join with planets who choir their delight (1917)

Source: Hamilton Fish Armstrong, ed. *The Book of New York Verse.* NY: G. P. Putnam's Sons, 1917.

288. **Walter Lippman** (1889–1974), American journalist, author, essayist

Robinson Crusoe, the self-sufficient man, could not have lived in New York. (1968)

Source: *Newsweek*. February 26, 1968.

289. **Raymond F. Loewy** (1893–1968), French engineer and industrial designer

New York is simply a distillation of the United States, the most of everything, the conclusive proof that there is an American civilization. New York is casual, intellectual, subtle, effective, and devastatingly witty. But her sophisticated appearance is the thinnest of veneers. Beneath it there is power, virility, determination and sense of destiny. (1964)

Source: Charles Hurd, comp. *A Treasury of American Great Quotations*. NY: Hawthorn Books, 1964.

290. **Stephen Longstreet** (1907–   ), American author and journalist

New York is a unique personality, continually shifting and alternating, becoming in each era a new and enchanting character, but often with agonizing and sinister undertones. It is a contradictory city, having its special virtues and certain personal aspects of social status—seeking of crimes, glories, and political hanky-panky, which have always fascinated the rest of the nation. (1975)

Source: Stephen Longstreet. *City on Two Rivers: Profiles of New York Yesterday and Today.* NY: Hawthorn Books, 1975.

291. **Pierre Loti** (1850–1923), French novelist, born Julien Viaud

But what a noisy place it is! . . . When I return from here [NYC] Paris will seem just a quiet old fashioned little town, with tiny, low houses, nor will any of its Fourteenth of July illuminations approach in brilliancy the phantasmagoric display that one may see in New York on any night of the year. (1912)

Source: Pierre Loti. *Letters of Pierre Loti to Madam Juliette Adam, 1882–1922.* Paris: Plon Nourrit, 1924 (title and quotation translated from the French).

292. **Edmund G. Love** (1912–), American author

New York attracts the most talented people in the world in the arts and professions. It also attracts them in other fields. Even the bums are talented. (1957)

Source: Edmund G. Love. *Subways Are for the Sleeping.* NY: Harcourt Brace, 1957.

293. **Suzan Elizabeth Lyman** (1906–1976), American author

From the beginning New York has coped with a variety of peoples, standards and customs. She has always possessed a lure that draws individuals from all over the world to seek their fortunes or to start a new life. . . . Visitors are constantly being warned "Don't judge the United States by New York City"—she's atypical . . . not only any other place in the country. (1975)

Source: Suzan Elizabeth Lyman. *The Story of New York: An In-formal History of the City from the First Settlement to the Present Day.* NY: Crown Publishers, 1975.

294. **Russell Lynes** (1910–   ), American author and art critic

Any real New Yorker is a you-name-it-we-have-it snob . . . whose heart brims with sympathy for the millions of unfortunates who through misfortune, misguidedness or pure stupidity live anywhere else in the world. (1965)

Source: *Town & Country* (magazine). August 1965.

295. **Jackie "Moms" Mabley** (1894–1975), American comedienne and vaudeville actress

Pollution is so bad in New York that I saw the Statue of Liberty holdin' her nose. (1973)

Source: *Black Stars* (magazine). May 1973.

296. **Mary M. McBride** (1899–1976), American author and biographer

One of us [McBride's coauthor] lives here [NYC] because she must, the other because she wouldn't live in any other place if you gave her a Cecil DeMille castle to go with it. One of us thinks New York is cruel and headless . . . the other claims that New York is so soft-hearted that beggars ride in limousines. (1931)

Source: Mary McBride and Helen Josephy. *New York Is Everybody's Town.* NY: Knickerbocker Press, 1931.

297. **James D. McCabe Jr.** (1842–1883), American author

This Great City, so wonderful in its beauty . . . is in all respects the most attractive sight in America, and one of the most remarkable in the world, ranking next to London and Paris in the extent and variety of its attractions. Its magnificence is remarkable, its squalor appalling. Nowhere else in the New World are seen such lavish displays of wealth, and such hideous depth of poverty. (1872)

Source: James D. McCabe Jr. *Lights and Shadows of New York Life.* NY: Farrar, Straus & Giroux, 1970 (facsimile of 1872 edition).

298. **Phillips McCandlish** (1927–   ), American author and journalist

The whole life and rhythm, the pulse and population of New York City is a living mosaic made up of millions of pieces, and the most anyone can know about them is fragmentary. (1974)

Source: Phillips McCandlish. *City Note Book: A Reporter's Portrait of a Vanishing New York.* NY: Liveright, 1972.

299. **Mary McCarthy** (1912–   ), American author and critic

The whole character of New York was changed by the appearance of these refugees who had a certain wisdom that was totally lacking in the crude society that was described in "The Group." (1968)

Note: *"The Group" refers to professional refugees who left Nazi Germany (e.g. Thomas Mann, Albert Einstein, Hanna Arendt and others.)*
Source: Carol Gelderman. *Mary McCarthy: A Life.* NY: St. Martin's Press, 1988.

300. **Diosdado Macapagal** (1910–   ), Filipino statesman and lawyer, was the Philippines' president from 1961 to 1964

New York is truly the City of Men's humanity in microcosm: reflecting the infinite variety as well as the infinite capacity for good and evil of the human race. (1964)

Source: *New York Times*. October 10, 1964.

301. **Carson Smith McCullers** (1917–1967), American author

Brooklyn, in a dignified way, is a fantastic place. The street where I live has a quietness and sense of permanence that seem to belong to the nineteenth century. . . . Comparing the Brooklyn that I know with Manhattan is like comparing a comfortable and complacent duenna to her more brilliant and neurotic sister. Things move more slowly here . . . and there is a sense of tradition. (1940s)

Source: Andrea Wyatt Sexton and Alice Leccese Powers, eds. *The Brooklyn Reader: 30 Writers Celebrate America's Favorite Borough*. New York: Harmony Books, 1994.

302. **Fred W. McDarrah** (1926–   ), American author and historian

On foot, on bicycles, in baby carriages or sight seeing buses, whatever conveyance carries them, everyone gathers here, cats and babies, artists and intellectuals, bankers and beatniks, Zen buddhists and swamis, shoe clerks and writers. . . . The Fountain is the heart of the [Greenwich] Village. (1963)

Source: Fred W. McDarrah. *Greenwich Village*. NY: Corinth Books, 1963.

◆ ◆ ◆

For 100 years, Greenwich Village has been the liveliest and most colorful community in New York. An exciting complex of interesting people, fascinating places, and dynamic ideas, the Village has the vitality of a metropolis, the intimacy of a neighborhood, and a personality of its own. (1992)

Source: Fred W. McDarrah. *The Greenwich Village Guide*. Pennington, NJ: A Capella Books, 1992.

303. **William McGonagall** (NDA), American poet and dramatist

Jottings of New York (poem)
Oh mighty city of New York! you are wonderful to behold,
Your buildings are magnificent, the truth be told,
They were the only thing that seemed to arrest my eye,
Because many of them are thirteen storeys high. . . . (1890)

Source: William McGonagall. *Poetic Gems: Selected from the Works of William McGonagall*. Dundee, Scotland: D. Winter, 1954 (reprint of 1890 edition).

304. **Jay McInerney** (1955–   ), American author

New York has always been too rich, too poor, too tall, too fast, too big, too loud, too dangerous. It is a city of excesses. And I can't seem to live anywhere else. Even at this late date, as the American Empire slouches into decline, New York seems to me the exact center of the world. (1988)

Source: Mike Marqusee and Bill Harris. *New York: An Illustrated Anthology*. Topsfield, MA: Salem House, 1988.

305. **Charles Mackay** (1814–1889), British author

It [Broadway] is a street *sui generis,* combining in itself the characteristics of the Boulevard des Italiens at Paris, and of Cheapside or Fleet Street in London, with here and there a dash of Liverpool and Dublin. It is longer, more crowded, and fuller of buildings than the Boulevard des Italiens: it is as bustling as Cheapside; and more than all, it has a sky above it as bright as the sky of Venice. Its aspect is thoroughly Parisian. (1857)

Source: Charles Mackay. *Life and Liberty in America, or Sketches of a Tour in the United States and Canada in 1857–8.* NY: Harper & Brothers, 1859.

306. **Claude McKay** (1890–1948), African American, Jamaican-born poet and author

Oh, to be in Harlem again after two years away. The deep-dyed color, the thickness, the closeness of it. The noises of Harlem. The sugared laughter. The honey-talk on its streets. And all night long ragtime "blues" playing somewhere . . . singing somewhere, dancing somewhere! Oh, the contagious fever of Harlem. Burning everywhere in dark-eyed Harlem. . . . (1940s)

Source: John Henrik Clarke, ed. *Harlem, USA.* NY: Collier Books, 1971.

307. **Mignon McLaughlin** (NDA), American author, born Neuhaus

A car is useless in New York, essential everywhere else. The same thing with good manners. (1966)

Source: Mignon McLaughlin. *The Second Neurotics Notebook.* Indianapolis, IN: Bobbs-Merrill, 1966.

308. **H. Marshall McLuhan** (1911–1980), Canadian author, educator

Of course, a city like New York is obsolete. . . . People will no longer concentrate in great urban centers for the purpose of work. New York will become a Disneyland, a pleasure dome. (1968)

Source: Tom Wolfe. *The Pump House Gang*. NY: Farrar, Straus & Giroux, 1968.

309. **Chris McNickle** (NDA), American historian and consultant

When New Yorkers elect a mayor they reduce the diversity of countless neighborhoods and millions of people to a single human point. To be mayor of New York requires the ability to reconcile the competing visions that the city's ethnic groups hold of the metropolis, at least in sufficient measure to earn the confidence of the majority. The political identity of the leader who does that is a telling barometer of New York's political climate. (1993)

Source: Chris McNickle. *To Be Mayor of New York: Ethnic Politics in the City*. NY: Columbia University Press, 1993.

310. **Norman Mailer** (1923–   ), American author and journalist

We [New Yorkers] were always the best and the strongest of the cities, and our people were vital to the teeth. Knock them down eight times and they would get up with that look in the eye which suggests that the fight has barely begun. (1969)

Source: *New York Times Magazine*. May 18, 1969.

♦   ♦   ♦

Brooklyn Heights is the most real place I've ever been in my life. I love to see the New York skyline from the Brooklyn side. You know all those postcards with the scenic view of

Manhattan? They're all shot from Brooklyn. And you know why? Because the photographers want an excuse to be in Brooklyn. (1992)

Source: Larry King. *When You're from Brooklyn, Everything Else Is Tokyo*. Boston: Little, Brown, 1992.

311. **George MacDonald Major** (1882–1903), American poet

Chinatown Visited (poem)
From sullen skies a cheerless rain
That floods the half-choked gutter drain,
Ramshackle houses, brick and wood,
Where hides disease with shroud and hood;
Worn doors, uncurtained window-panes
And mucky streets and garbage lanes.
And this is-this is Chinatown. (1899)

Source: George MacDonald Major. *Lays of Chinatown and Other Verses*. NY: H. I. Kimball, 1899.

312. **Bernard Malamud** (1914–1986), American novelist

I lived in Brooklyn until I got married and moved to Greenwich Village. . . . But Manhattan in those other days represented culture in the sense that it had something to show. . . . I thought of Brooklyn as a home town. (1971)

Source: *New York Times*. February 21, 1971.

313. **Seon Manley** (1921–   ), American author and editor

For some boys . . . the Village [Greenwich] was their introduction to New York itself, the city that would challenge them, where they would make their careers, where they would find themselves . . . New York has been a beacon . . . to people who wanted to be something, wanted to do something, wanted to feel the world with a little more intensity than other people, and perhaps even leave a mark on the world. (1969)

Source: Seon Manley. *My Heart's in Greenwich Village.* NY: Funk and Wagnalls, 1969.

314. **John F. Marion** (1922–   ), American author

The best and the worst [of NYC] are the two Cs—culture and crime. (1993)

Source: *New York* (magazine). December 20–27, 1993.

315. **Don R. Marquis** (1878–1937), American poet and humorist

New York (poem)
She is hot to the sea that crouches beside,
    Human and hot to the cool stars peering down,
    My passionate city, my quivering town . . .
    . . .
    Through the shaken length of her veined streets—
        She pulses, the heart of the world! (1917)

Source: Hamilton Fish Armstrong, ed. *The Book of New York's Verse.* NY: G. P. Putnam's Sons, 1917.

316. **Ralph G. Martin** (1920–   ), American author

Lincoln Center may be Pagliacci to you, but it's Richard Rodgers to me. (1971)

Source: Ralph G. Martin. *Lincoln Center for the Performing Arts.* Englewood Cliffs, NJ: Prentice Hall, 1971.

317. **Sister Maryanna** (1910–), American Catholic author, born Maryanna Childs

   For there is gaiety in this sprawling metropolis [NYC]. You hear it in the cheep of sparrows in the park, the laughter of the children in playgrounds, the banter of taxi drivers lightly insulting other motorists, and it is a truer gaiety than that which glitters in the night spots or theaters, where visitors so often seek it. (1960)

   Source: *New York Daily News*. April 9, 1960.

318. **Jackie Mason** (1930–), American comedian and a former rabbi

   The best [in NYC] is that it's the most exciting, vital, vibrant city around. But no matter where you go to enjoy it, you're bound to get mugged. (1993)

   Source: *New York* (magazine). December 20–27, 1993.

319. **Walter Matthau** (1920–), American actor and comedian

   In New York I get scared of talking to a telephone operator. People bark at each other. The word "please" is like some form of advanced voodoo. (1971)

   Source: Leonard L. Levinson, ed. *Bartlett's Unfamiliar Quotations*. Chicago: Cowles Book Co, 1971.

320. **Andre Maurois** (1885–1967), French novelist and critic, born Emile Herzog

   If in New York, you arrive late for an appointment, say "I took a taxi." (1950)

   Source: *New York Times*. August 13, 1950.

321. **Herman Melville** (1819–1891), American, NYC-born novelist, story writer, and poet

There is now your insular city of the Manhattoes, belted round by wharves as Indian isles by coral reefs—commerce surrounds it with her surf. Right and left, the streets take you waterward. Its extreme down-town is the Battery, where that noble mole is washed by waves, and cooled by breezes, which a few hours previous were out of sight of land. Look at the crowds of watergazers there. (1851)

Source: Herman Melville. *Moby Dick or the Whale*. NY: Norton, 1976 (reprint of 1857 edition).

322. **H. L. (Henry Louis) Mencken** (1880–1956), American editor and journalist

The life of the city, it must be confessed, is as interesting as its physical aspect is dull. It is, even more than London or Paris, the modern Babylon. . . . All the colossal accumulated wealth of the United States, the greatest robber nation in history, tends to force itself at least once a year through the narrow neck of the Manhattan funnel. To that harsh island come all the thieves of the Republic with their loot. . . . New York, indeed, is the heaven of every man with something useless and expensive to sell. (1925)

Source: H. L. Mencken. *Prejudices* (4th series). NY: Octagon Books, 1977 (reprint of 1925 edition).

♦ ♦ ♦

It is astonishing how little New York figures in current American literature. Think of the best dozen American novels of the last ten years. No matter which way your taste and prejudice carry you, you will find, I believe, that Manhattan Island is completely missing from at least ten of them, and that in the other two it is a little more than a passing scene unimportant to the main action. Perhaps the explanation is to be sought in the fact that very few authors of any capacity live in the town. (1927)

Source: H. L. Mencken. *Prejudices* (6th series). NY: Octagon Books, 1977 (reprint of 1927 edition).

323. **Eduardo Mendoza** (1943–   ), Spanish author and essayist

During two years I did not have any other idea than leaving it [NYC] and I moved earth and sky to get a transfer to Europe. But when the transfer finally arrived I realized that I could not leave New York. I was the first to be surprised . . . [how] that city so unexpectedly transformed me without realizing my own transformation. (1986)

Note: The author worked in 1970s at the United Nations headquarters when he arrived in NYC and the quotation refers to that period.
Source: Eduardo Mendoza. *Nueva York*. Barcelona: Ediciones Destino, 1986 (quotation translated from the Spanish).

324. **Aubrey Menen** (1912–   ), American author

The true New Yorker does not really seek information about the outside world. He feels that if anything is not in New York it is not likely to be interesting. (1959)

Source: *Holiday* (magazine). October 1959.

325. **David Michaelis** (1957–   ), American author and short story writer

New York's Fulton Street is the Vatican City of fish markets. (1984)

Source: *Manhattan, Inc.* (periodical). September 1984.

326. **Arthur Miller** (1915–), American dramatist and novelist

I'm at the end of the line; absurd and appalling as it may seem, serious New York theater has died in my life-time. (1989)

Source: *Times* (*London*). January 11, 1989.

327. **Henry Miller** (1891–1980), American, Brooklyn-born novelist

The City of New York is like an enormous citadel, a modern Carcasonne. Walking between the magnificent skyscrapers one feels the presence on the fringe of a howling, raging mob, a mob with empty bellies, a mob unshaven and in rags. (1939)

Source: Henry Miller. *The Cosmological Eye*. NY: New Directions, 1939.

◆ ◆ ◆

New York has a trip-hammer vitality which drives you insane with restlessness, if you have no inner stabilizer. . . . In New York I have always felt lonely, the loneliness of the caged animal, which brings on crime, sex, alcohol and other madnesses. (1941)

Source: Henry Miller. *The Colossus of Maroussi*. NY: New Directions, 1941.

◆ ◆ ◆

I am a patriot of Fourteenth Ward, Brooklyn, where I was raised. The rest of the United States doesn't exist for me, except as idea, or history, or literature. (1980)

Source: Andrea Wyatt Sexton and Alice Leccese Powers, eds. *The Brooklyn Reader: 30 Writers Celebrate America's Favorite Borough*. NY: Harmony Books, 1994.

328. **John Miller** (1666–1724), English military chaplain of New York

The number of Inhabitants in this province [NY] are about 3,000 families where almost one half are naturally Dutch, a great part English and the rest French. . . . As to their Religion they are very much divided, few of them intelligent and sincere, but the most part ignorant and conceited, fickle and regardless. . . . [Such is] the wickedness and irreligion of the inhabitants, which abounds in all parts of the Province and appear in so many shapes constituting so many sorts of sin that I can scarce tell which to begin with. . . . (1862)

Source: John Miller. *A Description of the Province and City of New York*. NY: W. Gowans, 1862.

329. **Terry Miller** (1947–   ), American novelist and theater producer

If Sheridan Square is the Heart of Greenwich Village, Washington Square is its soul. Even before a majestic marble arch rose here in the 1890s, a dignity of spirit existed in Washington Square. Like a human soul, it has intrigued generations of artists and writers, daring them to capture the elusive mystery of these 9½ acres in line and shadow, in photo and phrase. (1990)

Source: Terry Miller. *Greenwich Village and How It Got That Way*. NY: Crown Publishers, 1990.

330. **Jessica Mitford** (1917–   ), English author

Roaming the streets of New York, we encountered many examples of this delightful quality of New Yorkers, forever on their toes, violently, restlessly involving themselves in the slightest situation brought to their attention, always posing alternatives, always ready with an answer to an argument. (1960)

Source: Jessica Mitford. *Daughters and Rebels*. Boston: Houghton Mifflin, 1960.

331. **Eugene V. Mohr** (1929–), American author, university professor

Where do they [New Yoricans] belong? They have lost the land of their fathers and not yet found a way into the American mainstream. . . . And so they have opted to create, within inner city frontiers, their own society with its own music, language, ethics, politics and law. . . . New Yoricans however are not outlaws in the style of Weathermen. . . . Rather they see themselves as a separate but equal society with power to negotiate with the establishment. (1982)

Note: New Yoricans are Puerto Ricans of NYC. Weathermen was an American radical group of the 1960s.
Source: Eugene V. Mohr. *The New Yorican Experience: Literature of the Puerto Rican Minority*. Westport, CT: Greenwood Press, 1982.

332. **Marianne Moore** (1887–1972), American, Brooklyn-born poet

I like living here. Brooklyn has given me pleasure, has helped to educate me; has afforded me, in fact, the kind of tame excitement on which I thrive. (1961)

Source: Marianne Moore. A Marianne Moore Reader. NY: Viking Press, 1961.

333. **Paul Morand** (1888–1976), French author and diplomat

If the planet grows cold, this city [NYC] will nevertheless have been mankind's warmest moment. (1930)

Source: Paul Morand. *New York*. NY: Henry Holt & Co., 1930.

334. **Elsa Morante** (1916–   ), Italian author

This is not a city, it is the universe, the firmament, the viscera of the earth. You would love it. Millions of Anglo-Saxons, Italians, Spaniards, Chinese, Negroes, Puerto Ricans running around on the streets. Everyone returns your greetings as if they knew you . . . and all around, buildings like immense rocks, and cars like shooting stars. (1960)

Note: From a letter addressed to Pier Paolo Pasolini (1922– 1975), Italian movie producer
Source: Barth David Schwartz. *Pasolini Requiem*. NY: Pantheon Books, 1992.

335. **Ward Morehouse** (1898–1966), American author and Broadway critic

Broadway itself . . . was now cheapened and nightmarish. It was offering palm readings, and photos while-u-wait, live turtles and tropical fruit drinks, sheet music, nut fudge, jumbo malteds, hot waffles, ham and eggs, hot dogs and hamburgers. A screeching amusement park bedlam that was somehow without a Ferris wheel and a roller coaster, but presented shooting galleries, bowling alleys, guess-your-weight stands, gypsy tea rooms, rug auctions, electric shoeshines, dance halls. . . . (1949)

Note: The author describes Broadway of the 1930s.
Source: Ward Morehouse. *Matinee Tomorrow*. NY: McGraw-Hill, 1949.

336. **Ted Morgan** (1932–   ), American journalist and author, born Sanche de Gramont

In New York, I particularly like Chock Full O'Nuts for the world's best whole-wheat donut, for the menu, secure in its red-roofed plastic house, and for the sullen black waitresses, their names clipped to their brown dresses, like medals won on the field of battle. . . . (1978)

Source: Ted Morgan. *On Becoming American.* Boston: Houghton Mifflin, 1978.

337. **Christopher Morley** (1890–1957), American author

New York is Babylon. Brooklyn is the truly holy city. New York is the city of envy, office work, and hustle; Brooklyn is the region of homes and happiness. . . . [T]here is no hope for New Yorkers, for they glory in their skyscraping sins; but in Brooklyn there is the wisdom of the lowly. (1917)

Source: Christopher Morley. *Parnassus on Wheels.* NY: George Doran, 1917.

338. **George Pope Morris** (1802–1864), American poet

Dark Days (poem)
A stillness and a sadness pervade the City Hall,
And speculative madness has left the street of Wall
The Union Square looks really both desolate and dark
And that's the case or nearly, from Battery to Park. (1860)

Source: George Morris. *Poems of George Morris: With a Memoir of the Author.* New York: C. Scribner's Sons, 1860.

339. **James Morris** (1926–   ), Welsh journalist and author

Manhattan is one of the great art exchanges of the world, one of the great theater cities, one of the great fashion centers. Through New York, all the American philosophies, from the Jeffersonian to the Revivalist to the Hippy, have been shipped to other countries; through New York all the inventions of Europe, French hairdos or English plays or Italian Vermouth or German cars, are disseminated throughout the United States. (1969)

Source: James Morris. *The Great Port: A Passage through New York*. NY: Oxford University Press, 1969.

340. **Jan Morris** (1926–), Welsh journalist and author. Born as James Morris, but underwent a sex-change operation and now writes under name Jan Morris.

Chinatown, the Old Jewish Quarter, Harlem—they were the most evident and celebrated Manhattan's neighborhoods, But everywhere else on the Island [Manhattan] too racial enclaves of one kind or another were expanding or decreasing, fermenting or quiescent, lying low or asserting themselves, accepting the proposition of the Melting Pot or propagating its sociological rival of the time, Cultural Pluralism. (1945)

Source: Jan Morris. *Manhattan '45*. NY: Oxford University Press, 1987.

341. **Willie Morris** (1934–), American author

And it was to this city, whenever I went home, that I always knew I must return, for it was mistress of one's wildest hopes, protector of one's deepest privacies. It was half insane with its noise, violence, and decay, but it gave one the tender security of fulfillment. (1971)

Source: Willie Morris. *Yazoo: Integration in a Deep-Southern Town*. NY: Harper's Magazine Press, 1971.

342. **Toni Morrison** (1931–), African American author, Pulitzer Prize winner in literature

The New York Public Library is more than brilliant, more, even, than major. What we celebrate tonight is its necessity. New York City is unthinkable without it. (1995)

Note: From the toast written by Morrison to celebrate New York Public Library's 100th Anniversary on December 6, 1995.
Source: *New York Times,* December 7, 1995

343. **Samuel Morse** (1791–1872), American inventor of the telegraph and Morse Code

There is nothing new in New York, everybody is driving after money, as usual, and there is an alarm of fire every half hour, as usual, and the pigs have the freedom of the city, as usual, so in these respects at least, you will find New York as you left it. (1832)

Note: From a letter addressed to James Fenimore Cooper (1789–1851), American author
Source: Robert E. Spiller. *Fenimore Cooper: Critic of His Time.* NY: Russell & Russell, 1963.

344. **Robert Moses** (1888–1981), American public official and author

Unfortunately there are still people in other areas who regard New York City not as a part of the United States, but as a sort of excrescence fastened to our Eastern shore and peopled by the less venturesome waves of foreigners who failed to go West to the genuine American frontier. (1956)

Source: Robert Moses. *Working for the People: Promise and Performances in Public Services.* NY: Harper, 1956.

345. **Frank Moss** (1860–1920), American author and historian

The swirling currents that lave the shores of Manhattan Island, flowing in every direction, are reproduced in the human currents that eddy and rush through the streets of New York. The diversities of the City that are directly affecting their social affairs, and indirectly touching all their interests. . . . (1897)

Source: Frank Moss. *The American Metropolis: From Knicker-bocker Days to the Present Time.* NY: Peter Fenelon Collier, 1897.

346. **Patrick M'Roberts** (NDA), Wealthy Scottish traveler

The City is large, and contains a great many buildings, the public buildings and places of worship are generally very neat, and well finished, if not elegant. . . . The inhabitants are in general brisk and lively, kind to strangers, dress very gay, the fair sex are in general handsome, and said to be very obliging. (1774)

◆ ◆ ◆

Above 500 ladies of pleasure keep lodgings contiguous within the consecrated liberties of St. Paul's (Church). . . . Here all prostitutes reside, among whom are many fine well dressed women and it is remarkable that they live in much greater cordiality one with another than any nests of that kind do in Britain or Ireland. (1774)

Source: Patrick M'Roberts. *A Tour through Part of the North Provinces of America, Being a Series of Letters Wrote on the Spot in the Years 1774 & 1775* (ed. by Carl Bridenbaum). Philadelphia: Historical Society, 1935 (reprint of 1776 edition).

347. **Malcolm Muggeridge** (1903–1990), English author and journalist

I marveled once more at the Manhattan skyline, misty in the autumn light, exquisite in its unique, original way. The only architectural achievement of our time. (1957)

◆ ◆ ◆

The skyscrapers [of NYC] began to rise again, fraily massive, elegantly utilitarian, images in their grace, audacity and inconclusiveness, of the whole character of the whole people who produced them. (1957)

Source: Malcolm Muggeridge. *Like It Was: The Diaries of Malcolm Muggeridge* (ed. by John Bright Holmes). London: St. James' Place, 1981.

348. **Lewis Mumford** (1895–1990), American author and urban development critic

New York is the perfect model of a city, not the model of a perfect city. (1979)

Source: Lewis Mumford. *My Work Days*. NY: Harcourt, Brace, Jovanovich, 1979.

349. **Nicolas Nabokov** (1903–1978), Russian-American composer and author

I remember *not* being surprised or overwhelmed by New York. I found it the way I expected it to be: a kind of immense vertical mess (Edmund Wilson used to call it real estate gone mad) set upon a square horizontal order. (1975)

Source: Nicolas Nabokov. *Bagazh: Memoirs of a Russian Cosmopolitan*. NY: Atheneum, 1975.

350. **Gloria Naylor** (1950–   ), African American fiction author

There's something hypocritical about a city that keeps half of its population underground half the time; you can start believing that there's much more space than there really is — to live, to work. (1988)

Source: Gloria Naylor. *Mama Day*. NY: Ticknor & Field, 1988.

351. **Geoffrey Needler** (NDA), American university professor

[T]he reputed speech of Brooklyn . . . must be gleaned in the ephemera of the popular media: scores of dimly remembered radio scripts, mouldering newspaper gossip columns, vacuous joke books, and, of course, the daily sallies of tongue-in-cheek sportswriters who portrayed to a credulous public the intense linguistic distortion wrought mysteriously whenever Brooklyn and baseball were linked. (1977)

Source: Rita Seidan Miller, ed. *Brooklyn USA: The Fourth Largest City in America.* NY: Brooklyn College Press, 1977.

352. **Cathleen Nesbitt** (1888–1982), British theater and movie actress

Most human beings are driven to seek security and comfort. But there is another group that can only thrive on change and the unexpected of New York. (1972)

Source: Helen Hayes and Anita Loos. *Twice Over Lightly: New York Then and Now.* New York: Harcourt, Brace, Jovanovich, 1972.

353. **Byron Rufus Newton** (1861–1938), American journalist, NYC civil servant and author

Owed to New York (poem)
Vulgar of manner, overfed,
Overdressed and underbred
Heartless, Godless, hell's delight,
Rude by day and lewd by night;
. . .
A squirming herd in Mammon's mesh,
A wilderness of human flesh;
Crazed with avarice, lust and rum,
New York, the name's Delirium. (1906)

Source: *Best Loved Poems of the American People* (ed. by Hazel Felleman). NY: Doubleday, 1936.

354. **The** *New York Times* (1851–   ), American daily published by the New York Times Company, New York

If the park [Central Park] marks the geographical center of this densely packed island [Manhattan], it also marks a certain emotional core. This, after all, is where generations of New Yorkers have walked their dogs, pushed baby carriages, biked and skated, listened to music, thought deep thoughts and even married. For many, it was their first and last backyard. (1994)

Source: Editorial of September 21, 1994.

◆   ◆   ◆

"[I]n the 90's, New York has emerged as the most success-ful sports town in America. . . . The Yankees are the fourth local champion team of the 90's: the 1990 Giants won the Super Bowl, the 1994 Rangers and the 1995 Devils won the Stanley Cup. In the 90's, no other American city has teams that won three of the four major championships—World Se-ries, Super Bowl and Stanley Cup. And in the confusion, the 1994 Knicks were within a 3-pointer of winning the National Basketball Association title." (1996)

Note: October 26, 1996, the New York Yankees won the World Se-
ries championship by defeating the Atlanta Braves, retreiving
the title after 18 years. The victory was later celebrated on Oc-
tober 29, 1996, with a ticker-tape parade on Broadway, in
which more than 3 million New Yorkers participated.

Source: *New York Times,* October 28, 1996, p. C3.

355. *The New Yorker* (1925–   ), American monthly published in NYC

The two moments when New York seems most desirable, when the splendor falls all around and the city looks like a girl with leaves in her hair, are just as you are leaving and must say good-bye, and just as you return and can say hello. (1955)

Source: Editorial of January 11, 1955

356. **Anaïs Nin** (1903–1977), American (French-born) author

I miss the animal buoyancy of New York, the animal vitality. I did not mind that it had no meaning and no depth. (1934)

Source: Anaïs Nin. *The Diary of Anaïs Nin*, vol. 2 (1934–1939). NY: Swallow Press, Vol 2, 1967.

357. **Charlotte O'Brien** (1845–1909), Irish American author

New York life among the poor has one central distinguishing feature — namely, the fact that all live in tenements or in houses built on much the same principle. . . . In the typical tenement house the staircase passes up a well in the center of the house. It has no light from the open air, no ventilation; it is absolutely dark at midday except for such glasses over the doors of the flats, and possibly from a skylight at the top of the house. (1884)

Source: Charlotte O'Brien. *Selections from Her Writings and Correspondence.* Dublin: Mansel, 1909.

358. **Sean O'Casey** (1880–1964), Irish dramatist

The wide wonder of Broadway is disconsolate in the daytime; but gaudily glorious at night, with a milling crowd filling sidewalk and roadway, silent, going up, going down, between upstanding banks of brilliant lights, each building braided and embossed with glowing, many-coloured bulbs of man-rayed luminance. A glowing valley of the shadow of life. The strolling crows went slowly by through the kinematically divine thoroughfare of New York. (1952)

Source: Sean O'Casey. *Rose and Crown: His Autobiography*, vol. 5. NY: Macmillan, 1952.

359. **William O'Dwyer** (1890–1964), American lawyer and politician, NYC Mayor from 1946 to 1950

I tell you, there were times when as Mayor, I truly wanted to jump. You would look out over the city from some place high above, and you would say to yourself, "Good Jesus", it's too much for me. (1958)

Note: O'Dwyer refers to the stressful life and difficult decisions the mayor has to make.
Source: Philip Hamburger. *Mayor Watching and Other Pleasures.* NY: Reinhart, 1958.

360. **Frank O'Hara** (1926–1966), American poet and critic

[T]hat's the way New York is. You have to just keep tearing it down and building it up. Whatever they're building they'll tear that down in a few years. (1952)

Note: O'Hara refers to demolishing brownstones in NYC.
Source: Brad Gooch. *City Poet: The Life and Times of Frank O'Hara.* New York: Alfred Knopf, 1993.

361. **Frederick Law Olmsted** (1822–1903), American city planner, architect, philosopher, and journalist

The tenement house, which is the product of the uniform 200-foot wide blocks, is beginning to be recognized as the primary cause of whatever is peculiarly disgraceful in New York City politics. . . . It is a calamity more to be deplored than the yellow fever at New Orleans, . . . more than the fogs of London, the cold of St. Petersburg, or the malaria of Rome, because more constant in its tyranny. (1879)

Source: *A Biography of Frederick Law Olmsted.* Baltimore: Johns Hopkins University Press, 1973.

362. **James Oppenheim** (1882–1918), American poet and author

New York from a Skyscraper (poem)
Up in the heights of evening skies,
my City of Cities float,
In sunset's golden and crimson dyes:
and a great joy clutches my throat. (1914)

Source: *Songs from the New Age.* New York: Century Co, 1914.

363. **Laughton Osborn** (1809–1878), American poet and author

Five Points (poem)
. . .
Dogs, cats and children in one litter cry,
And mud-cak'd pigs encroach upon the sty.
Without, all wreck and nastiness; within,
Starvation, sickness, vermin, stench, and sin.
Such hives as still are found with even less room,
In Laurens Street, the Southern Side of Broom. (1838)

> *Note: Five Points was a poverty and crime-ridden section of NYC.*
> Source: Hamilton Fish Armstrong, ed. *The Book of New York Verse.* NY: G. P. Putnam's Sons, 1917.

364. **Collinson Owen** (1882–NDA), British author

A man who strolls in Hyde Park [London] after nightfall may possibly find himself in the police court next morning (It could largely depend on what kind of lady he met, and what sort of adventures attract him). But the man who strolled in Central Park after nightfall would almost certainly find himself in the morgue. (1929)

> Source: Collinson Owen. *The American Illusion.* London: E. Benn, 1929.

365. **Pier Paolo Pasolini** (1922–1975), Italian movie producer, director, and author

One thing does surprise me about your city . . . its deep humanism, the easy rapport we can have between people. Like Naples, in a sense. I even have the strange feeling that I have always been here. (1966)

> Source: *New York Times.* August 9, 1966.

◆ ◆ ◆

I'd like to be eighteen years old so as to be able to live a whole life here [NYC]. I am sorry not to have come here before, twenty or thirty years ago, to stay. It has never happened to me like this, so to fall in love with a place, except maybe Africa. (1975)

Source: *Europeo* (Italian publication). November 21, 1975.

366. **James Kirke Paulding** (1778–1860), American author and editor

Everybody [in NYC] appears to be in motion, and every thing else. The carriages rattle through the streets: the carts dance as if they were running races with them: the ladies trip along in all the colours of the rainbow: and the gentlemen look as though they actually had something to do. (1828)

Source: James K. Paulding. *The New Mirror for Travellers, and a Guide to the Springs*. NY: Self-published, 1828.

367. **Ann Petry** (1911–   ), African American author

No matter how you looked at it, it wasn't a good street to live on. It was a long cross-town street. Almost half of it on one side consisted of the backs of the three theaters on One Hundred Twenty-fifth Street—a long blank wall of gray brick. There were few trees on the street. Even these were a source of danger, for at night shadowy vague shapes emerged from the street's darkness, lurking near the trees, dodging behind them. (1970)

Note: Description of 125th Street in Harlem, New York. Presently the street is a central part of Harlem, substantially improved.
Source: Ann Petry. "In Darkness and Confusion," in *Harlem* (ed. John Henrik Clarke). NY: New American Library, 1970.

368. **Alex Phillips** (1900–1977), British actor and cameraman in Hollywood and Mexican movies

The feeling I have for this city is akin to sexual love. It lies here waiting like a mistress for her demon lover at the very beginning of the affair. (1972)

Source: Helen Hayes and Anita Loos. *Twice Over Lightly: New York Then and Now*. New York: Harcourt, Brace, Jovanovich, 1972.

369. **Sylvia Plath** (1932–1963), American poet

I have learned an amazing lot here [NYC]: the world has split open before my gaping eyes and spilt out its guts like a cracked watermelon . . . and the shift to NYC has been so rapid that I can't think logically about who I am or where I am going. I have been very ecstatic, horribly depressed, shocked, elated, enlightened, and enervated—all of which goes to make up living very hard and newly. (1953)

Source: Anne Stevenson. *Bitter Fame: A Life of Sylvia Plath*. NY: Viking Press, 1989.

370. **Edgar Allan Poe** (1809–1849), American poet, short story writer, and critic

Brooklyn . . . has, it is true, some tolerable residences; but the majority, throughout, are several steps beyond the pre-posterous. What can be more silly and pitiably absurd than palaces of painted white pine, fifteen feet by twenty?—and of such it is the boasted "city of villas". You see nowhere a cottage—everywhere a temple which might have been a Grecian had it not been Gothamite—a square box, with Doric or Corinthian pillars, supporting a frieze of unsea-soned timber. (1844)

Source: Julian Symons. *The Tell-Tale Heart: The Life and Works of Edgar Allan Poe*. NY: Harper & Row, 1978.

371. **Katherine Anne Porter** (1890–1980), American novelist and short story writer, Pulitzer Prize winner

I have long silent days, no parties, no alcohol, no theaters, no weekends on the country—what DO I have then? Life never seemed more brimmed up with the kind of tunes I like: New York is no problem to me nor ever was as you know. Let the visiting firemen battle with the place—I never knew a place easier to live in except Paris. (1950)

Source: Katherine Anne Porter. *Letters of Katherine Anne Porter* (ed. by Isabel Bayley). NY: Atlantic Monthly Press, 1990.

372. **Vladimir Posner** (1934–   ), American television commentator and journalist, formerly a Soviet broadcaster

New York City had changed in the thirty eight years of my absence. It had become even wealthier. You could smell the sweet, rotting aroma of money . . . but New York had also become poorer. I was stunned by the bag ladies, by the number of people living in the streets. . . . Back in the forties . . . there was no crack. Junkies were a rarity. There was Harlem, but there was no South Bronx. (1987)

Note: The author left NYC in 1949 with his parents for the Soviet Union, and returned in 1987 to settle in NYC again.
Source: Vladimir Posner. *Parting with Illusions*. NY: Atlantic Monthly Press, 1990.

373. **Ezra Pound** (1885–1972), American poet and critic

And New York is the most beautiful city in the world? It is not far from it. . . . No urban night is like night here. . . . Squares after squares of flame, set up and cut into aether. Here is your poetry, for we have pulled down the stars to our will. (1912)

Source: Humphrey Carpenter. *A Serious Character: The Life of Ezra Pound*. London: Faber & Faber, 1988.

◆ ◆ ◆

New York (poem)
My city, my beloved
Thou art a maid with no breasts,
Thou art slender as a silver reed.
Listen to me, attend me!
And I will breathe into thee a soul—
And thou shalt live for ever. (1916)

> Source: Hamilton Fish Armstrong, ed. *The Book of New York's Verse.* NY: G. P. Putnam's Sons, 1917.

374. **George Pozzetta** (1942–   ), American scholar, historian, author, and university professor

More important to the future development of Italian New York . . . were labourers, tailors, barbers, fruit vendors, confectioners, saloon keepers, vendors of plaster statuary, and other petty merchants. . . . These pioneers supplied much of the leadership and direction, for good or bad, that was manifested among Italians in New York until well into the twentieth century. (1972)

> *Note: Pozzetta was describing NYC in the 1850s.*
> Source: George Pozzetta. In *Little Italies of North America* (ed. by Robert Harney and J. Vilena Scarpaci). Toronto: Multicultural History Society of North America, 1972.

375. **George Prentice** (1802–1870), American poet, editor, and author

In New York City, the common bats fly only at twilight. Brick bats fly all hours. (1860)

> Source: George Prentice. *Prenticiana or Wit and Humor in Paragraphs.* NY: Derby and Jackson, 1860.

376. **Ida S. Primoff** (NDA), American song writer

> *To the First City of Our Land* (song)
> To the first city of our land
> With hearts and voices blending
> We sing the praize of Dutchmen day,
> We chant of English holding
> Thy civic growth we praise in song. . . . (1903)

> *Note: Music by Frank Damrosch (1859–1937). This was the official song of NYC before World War II. A slightly modified version was suggested in the 1960s, but in 1985 Mayor Ed Koch opted for "New York, New York"*
> Source: Frank Damrosch. *Songs of New York.* NY: C. Scribner's Sons, 1903.

377. **Brett Pulley** (NDA), American journalist

> New York is part of the latest technology wave. As a Mecca for writers, graphic artists, musicians and film makers, it is poised to become one of the country's centers for the emerging multimedia industry, which combines visual and audio elements like animation, video and music to create films, CD-ROMs, television programming and virtual reality. (1995)

> Source: *New York Times.* February 13, 1995.

378. **Michael Pye** (1946–), American author, historian, and journalist

> There were black whores on Seventh Avenue, and down in "Coontown" in what is now Soho, and up in Harlem; French whores on 43rd Street and around New York University. Whores around Columbia University . . . and whores on the Bowery . . . white whores for Chinatown, Italian whores on Mulberry Street in the heart of the slums, and Jewish whores on the lower East Side [who] sprawled indolently, their legs taking up half the pavement. (1991)

Note: Pye is describing NYC in the 1880s.
Source: Michael Pye. *Maximum City: The Biography of New York.*
London: Sinclair-Stevenson, 1991.

◆ ◆ ◆

You come to New York to be a writer, a painter, a performer;
it's a question of identity, not just work. You come for the
community of people who think the same way, for the pub-
licity, the support systems and the possibilities. You can
learn here. You can be judged by your peers here; you can
earn respect. There are far more comfortable cities to strug-
gle in, but only this one lives at the exact intersection of an
idea and a market.

Source: Michael Pye. *Maximum City: The Biography of New York.*
London: Sinclair-Stevenson, 1991.

379. **Anna Quindlen** (1953–   ), American author, journalist,
and columnist for NYT

[T]he truth about the cats may be that they fit into this city well
because they seem to possess some of the salient traits of New
Yorkers: a sleek self-assurance, a slight attitude of arrogance,
and unconcern with public opinion, a nose in the air. (1982)

Source: *New York Times.* January 6, 1982.

380. **Catherine M. Rae** (1914–   ), American author and critic

New York City of the 1840's was an incredibly dirty city,
and efforts to clean it up were only sporadic, usually spurred
by the outbreak of one infectious disease or another. The
poverty and squalor that so appalled Charles Dickens on his
visit in 1842 was everywhere and the number of Street Arabs
(homeless boys and girls) mounted. It was not until the fifties
that measures were taken concerning this growing army of
orphans and waifs . . . . (1984)

Source: Catherine M. Rae. *Edith Wharton's New York Quartet.* Lanham, MD: University Press of America, 1984.

381. **Ronald Reagan** (1911–   ), American actor, statesman, and U.S. President from 1981 to 1988

For millions of anxious immigrants, the forebears of countless millions of today's Americans, she [the Statue of Liberty] was the first glimpse of America. She was assurance of journey's end, safe harbor reached at last, and the beginning of a new adventure in a free and blessed land. For them she was a dream come true, the Lady with the Lamp, a warm welcome to a new life. (1986)

Note: From a speech celebrating the Statue of Liberty's Centenary in NYC.
Source: Richard Seth Hayden and Therry Despoint, eds. *Restoring the Statue of Liberty*. NY: McGraw-Hill, 1986.

382. **John Reed** (1887–1920), American journalist and poet

Proud New York (poem)
. . .
Manhattan, zones with ships, the cruel
   youngest of all the world's great towns,
Thy bodice bright with many a jewel,
   Imperially crowned with crowns (1919)

Source: Jack Alan Robbins, ed. *The Complete Poetry of John Reed*. Lanham, Md.: University Press of America, 1983.

383. **Mike Reynolds** (NDA), American comedian

Let me give you a tourist tip. If you want to go to New York, bring a camera there, because you'll see things you'll never see again. The first thing you'll never see again is your camera. (1990)

Source: Ronald L. Smith, ed. *Comedy Quote Dictionary*. NY: Doubleday, 1992.

384. **Ernest Rhys** (1859–1946), British poet, editor, and literary critic

New York as I recollect it, had a much sweeter smell in those days. . . . There was no disgusting gasoline to poison the air, and when one walked out early in the morning there was a floating breath of woodsmoke that vaguely recalled villages in Wales and Normandy. (1931)

Note: Rhys refers to NYC in the 1880s.
Source: Ernest Rhys. *Everyman Remembers*. NY: Cosmopolitan Corp. Books, 1931.

385. **Frank Rich** (1949–   ), American journalist, NY Times columnist

The New York Public Library . . . remains not only an institution that works but one that still upholds the old, tarnished faith that a great city might deliver great services to all its citizens . . . At its best, the library is a model of municipal intellectual and social service to the community, a shrine to culture high and low, and long before it was fashionable, a prime example of private-public financial partnership. (1995)

Note: Reference is made to New York Public Library on its 100th anniversary on December 6, 1995.
Source: *New York Times,* December 6, 1995.

386. **Joan Rich** (NDA), American author

It's true that really dedicated New Yorkers have the conviction that Manhattan is the world; furthermore that it's flat and if you go too far out of the Hudson River, you fall off.

It's understandable. For a genuine city dweller, New York *does* seem to have everything. (1964)

Source: Joan Rich. *How to Be a New Yorker*. Garden City, NY: Doubleday, 1962.

387. **Jacob Riis** (1849–1914), American journalist, author, and photographer

New York is, I firmly believe, the most charitable city in the world. Nowhere is there so eager a readiness to help, when it is known that help is worthily wanted. Nowhere are such armies of devoted workers, nowhere such an abundance of means ready to the hand of those who know the need and how rightly to supply it. (1890)

◆ ◆ ◆

Along the waterfronts, in holes of the dock rats, and on the avenues, the young tough finds plenty of kindred spirits. Every corner has its gang not always on the best of terms with the rivals in the next block, but all with a common programme: defiance of law and order, and with a common ambition: to get "pinched"; i.e. arrested, so as to pose as heroes before their fellows. . . . The gang is an institution in New York. (1890)

Note: The author was concerned about slum life and worked as a social worker in the slums.
Source: Jacob Riis. *How the Other Half Lives: Studies among the Tenements of New York*. Cambridge, MA: Belknap Press, 1970 (reprint of 1890 ed.).

388. **Moses Rischin** (1925–   ), American author focusing on Jews in America

The Jews of New York are the direct heirs of the Jewish Enlightenment and the great migration [1874–1914], the Lower

East Side and the great strikes in the needle trades, socialism and the settlements. To the extent that this American baptismal still operates in their lives, they retain a vivid sense of promise of a democratic community in a metropolis where few observers are inclined to be sanguine about such possibilities. (1962)

Source: Moses Rischin. *The Promised City: New York's Jews, 1870–1914*. Cambridge, MA: Harvard University Press, 1962.

389. **Rita** (1860–1938), British novelist, born Eliza Margaret J. Golan Humphreys

Society in New York is a curious admixture of "sets". There is first the wealthy Fifth Avenue set, then the wealthy Jewish set, then the professional middle-class set, then the intellectual set, then come various cults, or, as some call them "freaks". These are remarkable for some special fad, and that fad is trotted out and talked to death and made as much of a nuisance as people will stand. But American patience seems unlimited. (1910)

Source: Rita (pseud.). *America—Through English Eyes*. London: Stanley Paul, 1910.

390. **Cecil Roberts** (1892–1976), British author

It [NYC] is a city designed for pickpockets, the most romantic aspects of the city being on the summits of towering buildings where the architects burst into reminiscenses of Ur of the Chaldees, the Hanging Gardens of Babylon, the campaniles, domes and porticos of Italy and here and there the patios of Spain, the mosques and minarets of the East. (1947)

Source: Cecil Roberts. *And So America*. Garden City, NY: Doubleday, 1947.

391. **John Roebling** (1806–1869), American engineer, constructor of the Brooklyn Bridge and other bridges

The completed work [the Brooklyn Bridge], when constructed in accordance with my designs, will not only be the greatest bridge in existence, but will be the greatest engineering work of the continent, and of the age. (1867)

Note: From Roebling's proposal before the Brooklyn Bridge was approved.
Source: David McCullough. *The Great Bridge*. NY: Simon & Schuster, 1972.

392. **W. G. (William Garland) Rogers** (1896–1978), American author

By day the famous [Times] Square takes on the slack appearance of something somebody forgot to finish. . . . By night, however, it turns on the dazzling bright lights the world has read about and seen in the original or viewed in photos or on the screen; and it fills up with the uncountable autos and uncountable men, women and children. Where else on the entire earth can so many people have gathered?—Millions every week, hundreds of thousands for Election Night returns, a New Year's Eve, for celebrations of all sorts. . . . (1960)

Source: W. G. Rogers. *Carnival Crossroads: The Story of Times Square*. NY: Doubleday, 1960.

393. **Will (William Penn Adair) Rogers** (1879–1935), American actor, humorist, and author

One time here in New York, I played at a big benefit to get a Statue of Liberty for Russia. Now can you imagine Russia with a Statue of Liberty? We don't even know if they want one or not. If they do want one we will loan them ours. Ours has got its back turned on us at the present time, showing us that our liberty is behind us. (1928)

Source: Will Rogers. *The Autobiography of Will Rogers*. NY: Avon, 1979 (reprint of 1928 ed.).

◆ ◆ ◆

Hardly a day goes by, you know, that some innocent by-
stander ain't shot in New York City. All you got to do is to
be innocent and stand by and they're gonna shoot you. The
other day, there was four people shot in one day—four innocent people—in New York City. Amazing. It's kind of
hard to *find* four innocent people in New York. That's why
a policeman don't have to aim. He just shoots anywhere.
Whoever he hits, that's the right one. (1972)

Source: *Reader's Digest.* June 1972.

394. **Al Roker, Jr.** (1954–   ), African American television
weathercaster and show host

The Seaview Projects Complex, which towers over the Belt
Parkway in Canarsie [Brooklyn], epitomized the melting pot
flavor of Brooklyn. . . . The variety of nationalities who lived
there were all bonded by their lower middle-class status, yet
the enduring hope for most families, was owning their own
home. To achieve that goal, parents sacrificed and worked
very hard. . . . While there were occasional problems . . . it
was basically a harmonious environment where people
watched out for each other. (1991)

Note: Roker describes this section of Brooklyn as it was in the
1950s.
Source: Ralph Monti. *I Remember Brooklyn: Memoirs from Fa-*
mous Sons and Daughters. NY: Carol Publishing, 1991.

395. **Sigmund Romberg** (1887–1951), American composer and
conductor

Fifth Avenue (song)
Fifth Avenue, Fifth Avenue
Where fashions new are shown to you,

With all the latest styles on view
Each man or maid by fashion swayed
    there on parade. . . . (1915)

Source: NYPL. *Lincoln Center of Performing Arts Library*. Item MC "A World of Pleasure."

396. **Theodore Roosevelt** (1858–1919), American statesman, U.S. President from 1901 to 1909, and Nobel Prize Winner for Peace (1905)

Few commercial capitals have ever grown with more marvelous rapidity than New York. The great merchants and men of affairs who have built up her material prosperity, have not merely enriched themselves and their city; they have also played no inconsiderable part in the rapid opening up of the American continent during the present century, which has been rendered possible by the eagerness and far reaching business ambition of commercial adventures, welding the wonderful tools forged by the science of our day. (1895)

Source: Theodore Roosevelt. *New York, 1890–1895*. NY: Longmans Green, 1895.

397. **Charlie Rose** (1942–   ), American journalist, television host and producer

The best of New York? The celebration of potential. The worst of New York is the assault on dignity. (1993)

Source: *New York* (magazine). December 20–27, 1993.

398. **Joel Rose** (1936–   ), American author and editor

Murder proliferated at the Old Brewery [Five Points]. One long dark passage-way was known as Murderer's Alley, and as a wag of the day quipped, "was all that name implies". Cutthroat denizens lurked in every doorway, ready to spring, rob, and kill. Hundreds of children, born in windowless confines of the moldering tenement, allegedly did not see sunshine or breathe fresh air until their teens, because the much maligned monstrosity was as dangerous to leave as enter. (1987)

> *Note: Five Points was a poverty- and crime-ridden section of Manhattan (Lower East Side) and Rose describes what it was like in the 1880s.*
> Source: Joel Rose. *Between C & D: New Writing from the Lower East Side Fiction Magazine.* NY: Penguin Books, 1987.

399. **Judith Rossner** (1935–   ), American author

That's the New York thing, isn't it. People who seem absolutely crazy going around telling you how crazy they used to be before they had therapy. (1972)

> Source: Judith Rossner. *Any Minute I Can Split.* NY: McGraw-Hill, 1972.

400. **Henry Roth** (1906–   ), American, NYC-born novelist

All that day, as on all the day, her [NYC's] decks had been thronged by hundreds upon hundreds of foreigners, natives from almost every land in the world, the jowled close-cropped Teuton, the full-bearded Russian, the scraggly-whiskered Jew, and among them Slovak peasants with docile faces, smooth-cheeked and swarthy Armenians, pimply Greeks, Danes with wrinkled eyelids. All day her decks had been colorful, a matrix of the vivid costumes of other lands. (1934)

> *Note: Roth is describing the year 1907.*
> Source: Henry Roth. *Call It Sleep.* NY: R. O. Ballow, 1934.

401. **Jerry Rubin** (1938–1994), American radical anti-war activist, later businessman

Every person on the streets of New York is a type. The city is one big theater where everyone is on display. (1976)

Source: Jerry Rubin. *Growing (Up) at 37*. Philadelphia: M. Evans, 1976.

402. **Damon Runyon** (1884–1946), American author, journalist, and playwright

If I have all the tears that are shed on Broadway by guys in love, I will have enough salt water to start an opposition to the Atlantic and Pacific, with enough left over to run the Great Salt Lakes out of business. (1937)

Source: Damon Runyon. *More Than Somewhat*. London: Constable, 1937.

403. **Yves Saint Laurent** (1936–   ), French fashion designer

It has been so long since I've been here [NYC]. It is a beauty this city. It has always been a beauty, but it looks so clean and bright now. The people, also, they look wonderful. I am so glad to be here. (1994)

Note: Saint Laurent's last visit to NYC was in 1983.
Source: *New York Times*. September 20, 1994.

404. **G. A. (George Augustus) Sala** (1828–1895), British author

The shape of Manhattan island was like that of a sole, with its head in Harlem, and its tail at the Castle garden: the backbone being represented by Broadway, and the continuous line of ships fringing the wharves along the East River and the Hudson River respectively, figuring the lateral small bones of the fish. (1882)

Source: G. A. Sala. *America Revisited: From the Bay of New York*

to the Gulf of Mexico, and from Lake Michigan to the Pacific.
London: Vizettely, 1882.

405. **J. D. (Jerome David) Salinger** (1919–   ), American novelist and short story writer

I prayed for the city [NYC] to be cleared of people, for the gift of being a-l-o-n-e: which is the one New York prayer that rarely gets lost or delayed in channels, and in no time at all everything I touched turned to solid loneliness. (1964)

Source: J. D. Salinger. *Nine Stories*. Boston: Little, Brown, 1964.

406. **Edgar Saltus** (1855–1921), American author

Dante told of the inferno. He told too, of paradise. Manhattan may typify both. It represents other things also. The latter, mainly are superlatives. From the top floor of the Flatiron you get the idea of a few. On one side is Broadway. Barring trade routes, Broadway is the longest stretch on the planet. On the other side is Fifth Avenue. Barring nothing, Fifth Avenue is the richest thoroughfare in the world. (1958)

Note: Description of Manhattan at the turn of the century. The Flatiron Building, erected in 1902, is still in existence at the intersection of Fifth Avenue and 23rd Street.
Source: Grace M. Mayer. *Once Upon a City*. NY: Macmillan, 1958.

407. **Jean-Paul Sartre** (1905–1980), French philosopher, novelist, and playwright

Your [NYC's] streets and avenues have not the same meaning as ours. You go *through* them. New York is a city of movement. If I walk rapidly, I feel at ease. But if I stop for a moment I am troubled, and I wonder: why am I in this particular drugstore, Schrafft's, or Woolworth's, rather than any other drugstore, Schrafft's or Woolworth's from among the thousands just like this? (1946)

Source: *The New Yorker* (magazine). March 16, 1946.

408. **Siegfried L. Sassoon** (1886–1967), English author and poet

Storm on Fifth Avenue (poem)
A sallow waiter brings beans and pork . . .
Outside there's fury in firmament.
Ice-cream, of course, will follow; and I'm content.
O Babylon! O Carthage! O New York! (1921)

Source: *London Mercury* (British publication). April 1921.

409. **Emanuel Savas** (1931–   ), American educator, served as Deputy City Administrator of NYC in the 1970s

Genghis Khan conquered Asia with an army of only half the size of New York City's civil service.

Note: The reduction of NYC civil service bureaucracy remained a task for decades.
Source: *New York Times Magazine.* October 8, 1972.

410. **Charles Saxon** (1920–1988), American author

I particularly love Midtown Manhattan at twilight. As the embers and corals and purples light up the sky over Hudson, long shadows darken the streets. The crowds are gone . . . At twilight, New York can be frighteningly lonely, but magnificent. (1985)

Source: Roxie Munro. *Color New York.* NY: Timbre/Arbor House, 1985.

411. **Harold C. Schonberg** (1915–   ), American biographer and music critic

With its move to Lincoln Center, the Juilliard School has become the most impressive conservatory in the entire world . . . the Taj Mahal of conservatories, opulent, beautiful, domineering. (1971)

Source: Ralph Martin. *Lincoln Center for the Performing Arts*. Englewood Cliffs, NJ: Prentice Hall, 1971.

412. **Neil Sedaka** (1939–   ), American, Brooklyn-born singer and composer

Brighton Beach was a unique section of Brooklyn. In the 1940's it was a lower-to-middle class Jewish neighborhood where everyone looked the same and talked the same, families spoke Yiddish at home, had no contact with other neighborhoods, and thought that the whole world was Jewish. I wouldn't lay an eye on a WASP for months at a time. (1991)

Note: Sedaka refers to the 1940s when he grew up in Brighton Beach.
Source: Ralph Monti. *I Remember Brooklyn: Memoirs from Famous Sons and Daughters*. NY: Carol Publishing, 1991.

413. **George Segal** (1936–   ), American author

There's no room for amateurs [in NYC], even in crossing the streets. (1972)

Source: *Newsweek* (magazine). December 14, 1972.

414. **Roberta Seret** (1945–   ), American author

It takes knowledge, skill, and sense of humor to live in New York. But once you understand her and know where the pleasant places are, how to get there, what customs are imtant, what etiquette and traditions to follow, and how to ibout getting what you want, life in New York City can ruly exciting. (1983)

Source: Roberta Seret. *Welcome to New York: How to Settle and Survive in New York.* NY: American Welcome Services Press, 1989 (3rd ed.)

415. **Louis Sheaffer** (1919–), American author and editor

If writers, artists, and kindred spirits were attracted to Greenwich Village by cheap rentals, they fell in love with the area for less practical reasons: so many of the old houses, bearing witness to an elegant past, had large rooms with noble fire places; lower Fifth Avenue, starting Washington Square and the Arch, seemed like a boulevard in Paris; the little Italian restaurants where good red wine was an inseparable part of the meal, and non-Latins were introduced to the glories of garlic, added another cosmopolitan flavor. . . . (1968)

Note: Sheaffer refers to NYC in 1915.
Source: Louis Sheaffer. *O'Neill: Son and Playwright.* Boston: Little, Brown, 1968.

416. **Gail Sheehy** (1916–), American author

The upper East Side of Manhattan . . . is the province of Let's Pretend. (1971)

Source: Gail Sheehy. *Hustling: Prostitution in Our Wide Open Society.* NY: Delacorte Press, 1973.

417. **Richard Shepard** (1922–), American author and journalist

But here am I nitpicking when I know that my New York friends know much more about recently visited Paris, Prague, and Tokyo than they will ever know about their own city. After all, what's to know? They go to work and come home. New Yorkers are notorious for their ignorance of the town, although they are often leading experts on their own neighborhood. The double-deckers have not yet found

Queens Boulevard, Grand Concourse or Flatbush Avenue. Too bad, lots of real stories there. (1995)

Source: *New York Times,* August 21, 1995.

418. **Josiah Shippey** (1778–NDA), American poet

Columbia College (poem)
Columbia College! Alma Mater! Well
Do I remember, and the time could tell,
When first escaped from pedagogic rule,
To thee I came fresh from a grammar school
From five long years well stored, at all events
With English, Greek, and Latin rudiments. (1796)

Source: Josiah Shippey. *Specimens: Or Leisure Hours Poetically Employed on Various Subjects.* NY: J. B. Allee, 1841.

419. **Ian Shoales** (1949–   ), American author

New York—it's overpriced, it's dark, it's insular, it has absolutely no idea of what's going on in the rest of the country. The only thing it cares about is what it creates itself, and most of that is an illusion. (1988)

Source: Ian Shoales. *Ian Shoales' Perfect World.* (ed. by Merle Kessler). NY: Penguin Books, 1988.

420. **Kate Simon** (1942–   ), American author and memorialist

The writer of New York writes of swiftly rushing waters, or, to confuse a metaphor, rides an escalator with few still platforms, relentlessly propelled by an invention of Kafka. It is stimulating and discouraging: a report written two or three years ago may have the wistful charms of rememberances of things past, cherished and often unusable. Where is that wonderful Ukrainian restaurant like the kitchen of a generous peasant? . . . Evaporated into the wisps of nostalgia. (1971)

Source: Kate Simon. *New York, Places and Pleasures: An Uncommon Guide*. NY: Harper & Row, 1971.

421. **Neil Simon** (1927–   ), American, Bronx-born playwright

There are two million interesting people in New York, and only seventy eight in Los Angeles. (1982)

Source: *Dramatics* (magazine). September 1982.

422. **Isaac Bashevis Singer** (1904–1991), American novelist (Yiddish language), Nobel Prize winner in literature, 1978

Buildings will collapse, power plants will stop generating electricity. Generals will drop atomic bombs on their own populations. Mad revolutionaries will run in the streets crying fantastic slogans. I have often thought it would begin in New York [City]. This metropolis has all the symptoms of a mind gone berserk. (1982)

Source: Isaac Bashevis Singer. *Collected Stories of Isaac Bashevis Singer*. NY: Farrar, Straus & Giroux, 1982 (translated from the Yiddish).

423. **Betty Smith** (1896–1972), American, Brooklyn-born author and playwright

Serene was a word you cut put on Brooklyn, New York. . . . Somber, as a word was better. But it did not apply to Williamsburg, Brooklyn. Prairie was lovely and Shenandoah had a beautiful sound, but you could not fit those words in Brooklyn. Serene was the only word for it. Especially on a Saturday afternoon in summer. (1943)

Note: Smith refers to 1912, when she was a teenager in Brooklyn.

◆ ◆ ◆

There's a tree that grows in Brooklyn. Some people call it the Tree of Heaven. No matter where its seeds fall, it makes a tree which struggles to reach the sky. (1943)

Source: Betty Smith. *A Tree Grows in Brooklyn*. NY: Harper & Row, 1947 (reprint of 1943 ed.).

424. **Mortimer Brewster Smith** (1906–), American author, biographer and social historian

. . . I was schooled by the City of New York in the Nineteen Twenties. The city was a mute school-master that formulated no rules of attendance or grading, enforced no discipline and made no demands for attention, but offered a vast curriculum to anyone who wanted to take advantage of it . . . I am thankful that in those early formative years chance set me in New York and that I had the wit to pick and choose from the city's overflowing cornucopia some riches that stood by me. (1980)

Source: Mortimer B. Smith. *My School the City: A Memoir of New York in the Twenties*. Chicago's Regnery/Gateway, 1980.

425. **Jimmy Smits** (1955–), American, Brooklyn-born television and theater actor

When I look back on Brooklyn, I think of the neighborhoods there. To me, that's what Brooklyn's all about. It personifies, in a very positive way, the true definition of the word "neighborhood". People are affectionate about Brooklyn because of the people who live there, its history, and its character. It's the real world. (1991)

Note: Smits refers to 1960s Brooklyn.
Source: Ralph Monti. *I Remember Brooklyn: Memoirs from Famous Sons and Daughters*. NY: Carol Publishing, 1991.

426. **Raymond Sokolov** (1941–   ), American author specializing in cooking books

Manhattan is a narrow island off the coast of New Jersey devoted to the pursuit of lunch. (1984)

Note: Sokolov refers to the innumerable restaurants, coffee shops and street vendors found during lunchtime in Manhattan.
Source: *Wall Street Journal.* June 20, 1984.

427. **Susan Sontag** (1933–   ), American essayist and author

This city [NYC] is neither a jungle nor the moon. . . . In long shot: a cosmic smudge, a conglomerate of bleeding energies. Close up, it is a fairly legible printed circuit, a transistorized labyrinth of beastly tracks, a data bank for asthmatic voiceprints. (1978)

Source: Susan Sontag. *I, Etcetera.* NY: Farrar, Straus & Giroux, 1978.

428. **Muriel S. Spark** (1918–   ), British novelist

New York, home of the vivisectors of the mind, and the mentally vivisected still to be reassembled, of those who live intact, habitually wondering about their states of sanity, and home of those whose minds have been dead, bearing the scars of resurrection. (1973)

Source: Muriel Spark. *The Hothouse by the East River.* London: Macmillan, 1973.

429. **Robert Stephen Spitz** (NDA), American author and journalist

The Chelsea is undoubtedly one of Manhattan's most startling residences. A ten-story Victorian building on West Twenty-Third Street. . . . [U]nder one roof . . . lived the most incredible mix of oddballs and prodigies science has yet to observe: a who's who of rock stars, call girls, failed writers, drug dealers, ex-matinee idols, and assorted wackos. . . . (1989)

Note: Spitz refers to the 1960s.
Source: Bob Spitz. *Bob Dylan: A Biography*. NY: McGraw-Hill, 1989.

430. **Freya Stark** (1893–1993), British author

New York [City] . . . seemed to me one of the most exciting cities in the world: the blueness of the sky floated about its pencil buildings, and shops, taxis, all human affairs seemed to go in deep canyon-beds of natural erosion rather than among the excrescences constructed by men. It is the only town where one's looks are drawn all the time away from the ground into the sky. . . . (1943)

Source: Freya Stark. *Dust in the Lion's Paw: Autobiography, 1936–1946*. Levittown, NY: Transatlantic Arts, 1975 (reprint of 1962 ed.).

431. **Edmund Clarence Stedman** (1833–1908), American poet, author, and editor

Peter Stuyvesant's New Year's Call (poem)
Where nowadays the Battery lies,
   New York had just begun,
A new-born babe, to rub its eyes
   In sixteen sixty-one
They christen'd it Nieuw Amsterdam,
   Those burgers grave and stately
And so, with schnapps and smoke and psalm
   Lived out their lives sedately. (1860)

Note: Peter Stuyvesant (1610–1672) was the Dutch Governor of New Netherlands, before it became New York.

Source: Edmund C. Stedman. *Poems, Lyrical and Idyllic*. NY: C. Scribner's Sons, 1860.

◆ ◆ ◆

Pan on Wall Street (poem)
Where, hour, by hour, the rates of gold
   Outrival, in the ears of people,
The quarter-chimes, serenely tolled
   From Trinity's undaunted steeple. (1869)

Note: Stedman refers to Trinity Church and Wall Street.
Source: Edmund C. Stedman. *The Blameless Prince and Other Poems*. Boston: Fields, Osgood, 1869.

432. **Marjorie Steele** (1930–), American theater and movie actress

A City [NYC] composed of people who get acquainted with their neighbors by meeting them in Miami. (1988)

Note: Quote refers to NYC in 1960s.
Source: Eugene Brussells, ed. *Webster's New World Dictionary of Quotable Definitions,* 2d ed. Englewood Cliffs, NJ: Prentice Hall, 1988.

433. **R. Conrad Stein** (1937–), American author, titles for young readers

From the top of the Empire State Building, Manhattan looks like an army of glass-and-steel buildings. Indeed, three of the four tallest buildings in the world stand there . . . Viewed from above, the long rows of buildings form canyons through which flow rivers of toy-sized cars and people so small they resemble streams of ants. But Manhattan has an exciting human side . . . Its human drama can be discovered by taking a long walk—a walk that begins in the North and ends on the island's southern tip. (1989)

Source: R. Conrad Stein. *America the Beautiful: New York.* Chicago: Children's Press, 1989.

434. **John Steinbeck** (1902–1968), American novelist, Nobel Prize winner in literature, 1962

New York is an ugly city, a dirty city. Its climate is a scandal, its politics are used to frighten children, its traffic is madness, its competition is murderous. But there is one thing about it—once you have lived in New York and it has become your home, no place else is good enough. (1962)

Source: John Steinbeck. *Travels with Charlie in Search of America.* NY: Viking Press, 1962.

435. **Henry Steinmeyer** (1886–1980), American historian and author

[Staten Island] . . . combines advantages which, it is believed, are unrivalled in this country. Added to its proximity to the great commercial mart of the Western Hemisphere, it possesses a beauty of location, extent of prospect, and salubrity of climate, that will in vain be sought elsewhere. . . . It is separated from the City of New York by a distance of only five miles. . . . It is worthy of remark that these shores are uniformly free from the deposit of nuisance of any kind . . . fish and games of various descriptions are to be found in every direction. (1950)

Note: Steinmeyer refers to Staten Island in 1836. Quoted from a prospectus of 1836.
Source: Henry Steinmeyer. *Staten Island, 1524–1898.* Richmond Town, NY: Staten Island Historical Society, 1950.

436. **Isaac Stern** (1920–   ), American (Russian-born) violonist

Everywhere in the world, music enhances the hall, with one exception: Carnegie Hall enhances the music. (1985)

Source: *New York Times.* May 17, 1985.

437. **Wallace Stevens** (1879–1955), American poet

New York is a field of tireless and antagonistic interests—undoubtedly fascinating but horribly unreal. Everybody is looking at everybody else—a foolish crowd walking on mirrors. (1900)

Source: Holly Stevens, ed. *Souvenirs and Prophecies: The Young Wallace Stevens.* NY: Alfred Knopf, 1970.

438. **Robert Louis Stevenson** (1850–1894), British (Scottish-born) novelist, essayist, and poet

As I drew near New York [City] I was first amused, and then somewhat staggered, by the cautious and grisly tales that went around. You would have thought we were to land upon a cannibal island. You must speak to no one in the streets, as they would not leave 'til you were rooked and beaten. You must enter a hotel lobby with military precautions; for the least you had to apprehend was to awake the next morning without money and baggage, or necessary raiment, a lone fork in the bed: and if the worst befell, you would instantly and mysteriously disappear from the ranks of mankind. (1894)

Source: Robert Louis Stevenson. *The Amateur Emigrant: The Silverado Squatters.* NY: C. Scribner's Sons, 1905 (reissued in later editions).

439. **Bayrd Still** (1906–), British historian and author

More than ever before . . . there was the sense of New York as a great international city to which all the ends of the world had come. London used to be like that, but somehow one has forgotten it. . . . Coming from that sort of London . . . in the old days, New York had seemed just American. Now it was the centre of the world. (1956)

Note: Still's impressions after a ten year absence from NYC.
Source: Bayrd Still. *Mirror for Gotham: New York as Seen by Contemporaries from Dutch Days to the Present.* NY: Washington University Press, 1956.

440. **Clyfford Still** (1904–1980), American author

. . . that [NYC] miasma of evil, culture, quacks and charlatans. (1971)

Source: *New York Times.* January 20, 1971.

441. **Rex Todhunter Stout** (1886–1975), American author

I like to walk around Manhattan, catching glimpses of its wild life, the pigeons and cats and girls. (1956)

Source: Rex T. Stout. *The Witnesses.* NY: Viking Press, 1956.

442. **George Templeton Strong** (1820–1875), American, NYC-born businessman, lawyer, and philanthropist

People talk of the pride a New Yorker must feel in this great city! To be a citizen of New York is a disgrace. A domicile on Manhattan Island is a thing to be confessed with apologies and humiliation. The New Yorker belongs to a community worse governed by lower and baser blackguard scum than any city in the Western Christendom, or in the world, so far as I know. . . . (1868)

Note: Strong refers to NYC's corrupt political administration under William Tweed (1823–1878), also known as "Boss Tweed."
Source: George Strong. *The Diary of George Strong* (ed. by Allan Nevins). NY: Macmillan, 1952.

443. **Simeon Strunsky** (1879–1948), American author

New York has more hermits than will be found in all forests, mountains and deserts of the United States. (1944)

♦ ♦ ♦

The thing which in the subway [NYC] is called congestion is highly esteemed in the night spots as intimacy. (1944)

Source: Simeon Strunsky. *No Mean City.* NY: Dutton, 1944.

444. **Betty Lee Sung** (1924–), Chinese American author and teacher

At the moment, everyone you talk to in Chinatown [NYC] feels impotent and helpless about the gang situation. The people will express their fears. They are indignant. They will voice their concerns, but if actually confronted with gang extortions or muggings, they submit. They hand over the money without reporting it to the police or making a fuss. They hurry in Chinatown to do their errands and as quickly depart. (1977)

Source: Betty Lee Sung. *Gangs in New York's Chinatown.* Washington, DC: Office of Child Development, Department of Health, Education and Human Welfare, 1977.

445. **Horace Sutton** (1919–), American author

The pneumatic noisemaker is becoming the emblematic Sound of New York [NYC], the way the bells of Big Ben are the Sound of London. (1961)

Source: *Saturday Evening Post.* March 11, 1961.

446. **Gay Talese** (1932–   ), American author

New York, where 250 people die each day, and where the living dash for empty apartments. . . . Where on page 29 of this morning's newspaper are pictures of the dead; on page 31 are pictures of the engaged; on page one are pictures of those who are running the world, enjoying the lush years before they land back on page 29. (1961)

Source: Gay Talese. *New York: A Serendipiter's Journey*. NY: Harper & Row, 1961.

◆ ◆ ◆

New York is a city of things unnoticed. It is a city with cats sleeping under parked cars, two stone armadillos crawling up St. Patrick's Cathedral, and thousands of ants creeping on top of the Empire State Building . . . New York is a city for eccentrics and a center for odd bits of information. New Yorkers blink twenty-eight times a minute, but forty when tense. (1970)

Source: Gay Talese. *Fame and Obscurity: Portraits by Gay Talese*. NY: World Publishing Co., 1970.

447. **Peter Il'ich Tchaikovsky** (1840–1893), Russian composer

Compared with Paris, where at every approach, in every stranger's kindness one feels an attempt at exploitation, the frankness, sincerity and generosity of this city [NYC], its hospitality without hidden motives and its eagerness to oblige and win approval, are simply astonishing and, at the same time, touching. (1891)

◆ ◆ ◆

My concert [at Carnegie Hall] went excellently. . . . The enthusiasm was such as I never succeeded in arousing even in Russia. They called me out endlessly but especially dear to me was the enthusiasm of the orchestra. (1891)

Note: Tchaikovsky refers to his final appearance in the United States on May 9, 1891.
Source: Petr Il'ich Tchaikovsky. *The Diaries of Tchaikovsky* (transl. from the Russian by Wladimir Lakond). NY: W. W. Norton, 1945.

448. **William Makepeace Thackeray** (1811–1863), English author

There is some electric influence in the air & sun here [NYC] which we don't experience on our side of the globe. Under this Sun people can't sit still people can't ruminate over their dinners dawdle in their studies and be lazy and tranquil — they must keep moving, rush from one activity to another, jump out of sleep and to their business, have lean eager faces. . . . (1855)

Source: W. M. Thackeray. *The Letters and Private Papers of William Makepeace Thackeray* (ed. by Gordon R. Ray). Cambridge, MA: Harvard University Press, 1946.

449. **Dylan Thomas** (1914–1953), Welsh poet and author

There seems at first sight to be no reality at all in the life here [NYC]: it is all an enormous facade of speed and efficiency and power behind which millions of little individuals are wrestling, in vain, with their own anxieties. (1950)

Note: From a letter Thomas wrote to his parents.
Source: John Ackerman. *Dylan Thomas: His Life and Work.* London: Oxford University Press, 1965.

450. **Piri Thomas** (1928–   ), Puerto Rican American novelist and short story writer

In the day time Harlem looks kinda dirty and the people a little drab and down. But at night, man, it's a swinging place, especially Spanish Harlem. The lights transform everything into life and movement and blend the different colors into a magic cover-all that makes the drabness and garbage, wailing kids and tired people invisible. Shoes and clothes that by day look beat and worn out, at night take on a reflected splendor that the blazing multi-colored lights burn on them. . . . (1967)

Source: Piri Thomas. *Down These Mean Streets.* NY: Alfred Knopf, 1967.

451. **Henry David Thoreau** (1817–1862), American poet, essayist, and naturalist

You must not count much upon what I can do or learn in New York. . . . Everything there disappoints me but the crowd. . . . You don't know where any respectability inhabits. It is in the crowd in Chatham Street. . . . The crowd is something new, and to be attended to. It is worth a thousand Trinity Churches and Exchanges. . . . (1843)

Source: Henry Thoreau. *Journal, 1837–1844.* Princeton, NJ: Princeton University Press, 1981 (John Broderick, general editor).

◆ ◆ ◆

The whole island [Staten Island] is like a garden, and affords a very fine scenery. In front of the house is a very extensive wood; beyond which is the sea, whose roar I can hear all night long, when there is a wind. . . . There are always some vessels in sight—ten, twenty, or thirty miles off—and Sunday before last, there were hundreds in long procession, stretching from New York to Sandy Hook, and far beyond. . . . (1843)

Source: Henry Steinmeyer. *Staten Island, 1524–1898.* Richmond Town, NY: Staten Island Historical Society, 1950.

452. **James Thurber** (1894–1961), American humorist, illustrator, and author

We all know that the theater and every play that comes to Broadway have within themselves, like the human being, the seed of self-destruction and the certainty of death. The thing is to see how long the theater, the play, and the human being can last in spite of themselves. (1960)

Source: *New York Times.* February 21, 1960.

453. **Y. A. (Yelberton Abraham) Tittle** (1926–), American football player

You only know what it's like to play around here [NYC] if you played somewhere else first. This is the city for an athlete. (1974)

Source: Y. A. Tittle. *Quarterbacks Have All the Fun.* Chicago, IL: Playboy Press, 1974.

454. **Alexis de Tocqueville** (1805–1859), French historian, political scientist, and politician

When I arrived for the first time at New York, by that part of the Atlantic Ocean which is called the East River, I was surprised to perceive along the shore, at some distance from the city, a number of little palaces of white marble, several of which were of classic architecture. When I went next day to inspect more closely . . . I found that its walls were of whitewashed brick, and its columns of painted wood. All the edifices that I admired the night before were of the same kind. (1840)

Source: Alexis de Tocqueville. *Democracy in America* (Second part: 1805–1859). Garden City, NY: Anchor Books, 1969 (reprint of 1840 ed.).

455. **Boris Todrin** (1915–), American author and poet

Brooklyn is a province. Although it lies but across the river from what is the most metropolitan of all cities, and is in fact a borough of it, one may as well hail from Hoosick Falls (N.Y.) or Possum Trot (Newark) as from Brooklyn. (1944)

Note: Todrin compares Brooklyn to other small towns.
Source: Boris Todrin. *Out of These Roots.* Caldwell, ID: Caxton Printers, 1944.

456. **Lily Tomlin** (1936–), American stage and movie actress and comedian

Being a New Yorker is never having to say you're sorry. (1992)

Source: Ronald L. Smith, ed. *Comedy Quote Dictionary.* NY: Doubleday, 1992.

457. **Herbert Beerbohm Tree** (1853–1917), British author

In New York the earth seems to spin more quickly round its axis. (1916)

Source: *The Times (London).* September 9, 1916.

458. **Anthony Trollope** (1815–1882), English novelist

I have two faults to find with it [NYC]. In the first place, there is nothing to see; in the second place, there is no mode of getting about to see anything. (1862)

Source: Anthony Trollope. *North America* (ed. by Donald Smalley). NY: Alfred Knopf, 1951 (reprint of 1862 ed.).

459. **Frances Trollope** (1780–1863), British author

New York . . . appeared to us . . . a lovely and noble city. . . . It seemed perhaps more beautiful, more splendid, and more refined than it might have done, had we arrived directly from London; but making every allowance for this, I must still declare that I think New York one of the finest cities I ever saw, and as much superior to every other in the Union (Philadelphia not excepted), as London to Liverpool, or Paris to Rouen. . . . (1831)

Source: Frances Trollope. *Domestic Manners of the Americans.* London: Whittaker, Treacher, 1832 (reissued in later editions).

460. .**Leon (Lev) Trotsky** (1879–1940), Russian Communist leader, rival of Lenin, born Lev Davidovich Bronstein

Here I was in New York, city of prose and fantasy, of capitalist automatism, its streets a triumph of cubism, its moral philosophy that of the dollar. New York impressed me tremendously because, more than any other city in the world, it is the fullest expression of our modern age. (1930)

Source: Leon Trotsky. *My Life.* Gloucester, MA: P. Smith, 1976 (Russian version and first translation originally appeared in 1930).

461. **Mark Twain** (1835–1910), American novelist and humorist, born Samuel Clemens

They do not treat women with as much deference in New York [NYC] as we of the provinces think they ought. This is painfully apparent in the street cars . . . the overcrowding of the cars has impelled men to adopt the rule of hanging onto a seat when they get it, though twenty beautiful women came in and stood in their midst. That is going back toward original barbarism, I take it. (1861)

♦ ♦ ♦

I have at last, after several month's experience, made up my mind that it [NYC] is a splendid desert—a doomed and steepled solitude, where a stranger is lonely in the midst of a million of his race. A man walks his tedious miles through the same interminable street every day, elbowing his way through a buzzing multitude of men, yet never seeing a familiar face, and never seeing a strange one the second time. . . . [E]very man seems to feel that he has got the duties of two lifetimes to accomplish in one. (1867)

Source: Mark Twain. *Twain's Travels with Mr. Brown* (ed. by Franklyn Walker and Ezra Dane). NY: Alfred Knopf, 1940.

462. **Kenneth Tynan** (1927–1980), British playwright and theater critic

And there, unmistakably it is: the familiar Manhattan look: A pettish, slightly resentful frown, as if a great promise had somehow not quite been fulfilled. In the midst of prosperity, people look as if they had been robbed. (1960)

Source: Kenneth Tynan. *Tynan Right and Left: Plays, Films, People, Places and Events.* NY: Atheneum, 1967.

◆ ◆ ◆

Coming to New York from the muted mistiness of London, as I regularly do, is like traveling from a monochrome antique shop to a Technicolor bazaar. (1960)

Source: *Holiday* (magazine). December 1960.

463. **Lloyd Ultan** (1929–), Bronx-born historian and author

Beautiful Bronx . . . it was not uncommon for Irish children to play with Italian children, for Jew to be in the same school as gentile, for black to be friend with white. Yet in the midst of this growing cosmopolitanism, each family lived in a little village called neighborhood, and each neighborhood was usually dominated by one ethnic group which determined the flavor of life. . . . (1979)

Note: Quote refers to Bronx during 1920s–1950s.

Source: Lloyd Ultan. *The Beautiful Bronx* (1920–1950). New Rochelle, NY: Arlington House Publications, 1979.

464. **David Thomas Valentine** (1801–1869), American historian and author

New York is one of the most social places on the continent. The men collect themselves into weekly evening clubs. The ladies, in winter, are frequently entertained, either at concerts of music or assemblies, and make a very good appearance. They are comely and dress well, and scarce any of them have distorted shapes. (1853)

Note: Description refers to the middle of 18th-century New York.
Source: David T. Valentine. *History of the City of New York*. NY: G. P. Putnam, 1853.

465. **Bernardo Vega** (1885–NDA), Puerto Rican American politician (originally cigar maker) and author

We saw the lights of New York even before the morning mist rose . . . the excitement grew the closer we got to the docks. We recognized the Statue of Liberty in the distance. . . . In front of us rose the imposing sight of skyscrapers— the same skyline we had admired so often on postcards. Many of the passengers had only heard talk of New York and stood with their mouths open, spellbound. . . . We sighed as we set foot on solid ground, there, gaping before us, jaws of the iron dragon: the immense New York metropolis. (1914)

Source: Bernardo Vega. *Memoirs of Bernardo Vega* (transl. from the Spanish by Juan Flores). NY: Monthly Review Press, 1984.

466. **Giovani da Verrazano** (1485?–1528), Italian skipper of the ship *Delfina,* financed by King Francis I of France

Therefore, we took the boat and entering the river, we found the country [Manhattan] on its banks well peopled, the inhabitants not different from others being dressed out with feathers of birds of different colours. They came toward us with evident delight, raising loud shouts of admiration, and showing us where we could most securely land with our boat. (1524)

> *Note: Excerpt from Verrazano's diary recorded in May 1524; this was the first encounter between Europeans and Native Americans in NYC's history.*
> Source: Henry Moscow. *The Street Book: An Encyclopedia of Manhattan's Street Names and Their Origins.* NY: Hangstrom Co., 1978.

467. **Victor Vinde** (1903–   ), Swedish journalist and author

New York is a great world capital. It is varied, capricious, brutal and hard. It is alarmingly crowded and indescribably beautiful. . . . New York is not America, but it is part of America, something of that which is in the process of being shaped and developed, throughout the vast continent. New York still lives in the Babylonian confusion of tongues. . . . New York is both in the van of America and on the side of America. (1942)

> Source: Victor Vinde. *Amerika: Slar Still.* Stockholm: P. A. Nortsted & Soner, 1943 (quotation translated from the Swedish).

468. **Dan Wakefield** (1932–   ), American author

There are Puerto Ricans living in almost every part of Manhattan and yet most often they remain in isolation—their settlements soon become crowded ghettos. Spanish Harlem is not the only one of these—it is merely the oldest and the largest . . . the newer ones are being created every day as older residents react with the fear that greeted so many strangers in the past crying in dismay that Puerto Ricans are "taking over" and running away to some other spot. (1957)

Source: Dan Wakefield. *Island in the City: The World of Spanish Harlem.* NY: Arno Press, 1975 (reprint of 1957 ed.).

469. **Andy Warhol** (1930–1987), American artist and filmmaker

If you're a Rockefeller, New York is really your town. Can you imagine? (1975)

Source: Andy Warhol. *The Philosophy of Andy Warhol (From A to B to Back Again).* NY: Harcourt, Brace, Jovanovich, 1975.

470. **Charles Dudley Warner** (1829–1900), American author, travel descriptions, biographies

The shop signs were in foreign tongues; in some streets all Hebrew. On chance newstands were displayed papers in Russian, Bohemian, Arabic, Italian, Hebrew, Polish, German—none in English . . . The sidewalks and the streets swarmed with noisy dealers . . . It was not easy to make one's way through the stands and push-carts and the noisy dickering buyers and sellers . . . The houses seemed bursting with humanity . . . In the damp basements were junk dealers, rag pickers, goose-pickers. (1895)

Note: Description of the Lower East Side in New York at the end of the 19th century.
Source: Charles D. Warner. *The Golden House: A Novel.* NY: Harper, 1895.

471. **Grace Watson** (1926?–), African American lawyer (NYC-born); Director of Volunteers in Education in the 1970s

Of course I'll return to New York. It's my home. Is there any place else? I'd rather be a lamppost on Seventh Avenue than a queen in another country. (1971)

Note: Watson made this statement when she left NYC temporarily for Washington to lead the Volunteers in Education.
Source: *New York Times.* May 7, 1971.

472. **Robert Weaver** (1907–   ), American economist, U.S. Secretary of Housing and Urban Development from 1966 to 1969

New York is where you can get the best cheap meal and the lousiest expensive meal in the country. (c. 1966)

Source: Ronald L. Smith. *The Comedy Quote Dictionary.* NY: Doubleday, 1992.

473. **Bruce Weber** (1942–   ), American author and journalist

Rockefeller Center seems more an artificial or even imaginary city than part of a real one. Its aura is more Emerald City than New York as if the 63-year-old site—perhaps the world's most famous urban development— . . . were not in Midtown Manhattan between Fifth Avenue and Avenue of Americas, but in the end of Yellow Brick Road. To spend a day there . . . is to witness the Christmas season as Dorothy saw Oz, with amazement, giddiness, some delight in its saccharine pleasures, and the genuine hopefulness that Christmas, like a wizard, will put everything right. (1995)

Source: *New York Times,* December 15, 1995.

474. **Moses Weinberger** (1854–1940), NYC rabbi and author

In those days . . . in New York [City] begging was the best work there was . . . begging was a nice, pleasant and most wonderful experience—especially in the blessed city of New York, where more Jews live in a single block than in an entire large city in Poland, and more in one house than in the whole villages in Lithuania and Hungary. A beggar in New

York could carry on his business in a simple and honorable manner, without expending a great deal of effort . . . he could be a big shot, a respectable person in the community. . . . (1887)

Note: Refers to Jews in New York City. Some were beggars, and considered it an honorable occupation.
Source: Moses Weinberger. *People Walk on Their Head: Moses Weinberger's Jews and Judaism in New York.* NY: Holmes and Meier, 1982.

475. **Ralph Foster Weld** (1888–NDA), American historian of Brooklyn

New Netherlands was a rough, tough trading outpost. Fortune seekers of all descriptions and many races had been drawn to it, adventurers whose only object was to get from the Indians the skin of the mink and the beaver, which were so easily converted into great wealth when sold in Europe. No colony could be built securely out of such material. Permanent settlers were needed. . . . It was Brooklyn's destiny to help save New Netherlands by becoming a prosaic farm community, a region of plain *boers* and *bowers.* (1950)

Note: New Netherlands was the name by which NYC was known under Dutch administration in the seventeenth century; the name was changed to New York under the English
Source: Ralph Foster Weld. *Brooklyn Is America.* NY: AMS Press, 1967 (reprint of 1950 ed.).

476. **George Weller** (1907–), American author, Pulitzer Prize winner (1943)

If you are confused ask somebody. New Yorkers are very helpful. However, the first person you ask will give you the wrong answer. So ask loudly enough that others will overhear and make corrections. New Yorkers love to correct each other. (1977)

Source: Mike Edelhart and James Tinen, eds. *America the Quotable*. NY: Facts on File, 1983.

477. **H. G. (Herbert George) Wells** (1866–1946), English novelist and historian

My first impressions of New York are enormously to enhance the effect of . . . material progress . . . as something inevitable and inhuman, as a blindly furious energy of growth that must go on. . . . [T]he skyscrapers that are the New Yorker's perpetual boast and prise rise up to greet one . . . in a clustering group of tall irregular crenelations, the strangest crown that ever a city wore. . . . (1906)

Source: H. G. Wells. *The Future of America*. NY: Harper & Brothers, 1906.

◆ ◆ ◆

Noise and human hurry and vastness of means and collective result, rather than any vastness of achievements, is the pervading quality of New York. (1906)

◆ ◆ ◆

To Europe she [NYC] was America, to America she was the gateway of the earth. But to tell the story of New York would be to write a social history of the world. (1908)

Source: H. G. Wells. *The War in the Air; In the Days of the Comet; The Food of the Gods*. NY: Dover Publications, 1963.

478. **Morris Robert Werner** (1897–1981), NYC-born author

I am one of the three people who were born in New York, and I have lived here the better part of sixty years. I don't even want to live anywhere else, though I wouldn't mind revisiting Paris, London, and Venice. New York gives me largesse, stimulation and privacy. It is the best place in the world to work for a man who knows when to go to bed and as good a place as any to play almost any game. (1956)

Source: Morris R. Werner. *It Happened in New York.* NY: Coward-McCann, 1956.

479. **Glenway Wescott** (1901–), American author

Metropolis: New Yorkers who live in houses envy New Yorkers who live in apartments; New Yorkers who live in apartments envy New Yorkers who live in hotels; New Yorkers who live in hotels envy New Yorkers who live in hospitals, and vice versa, and ring-round rosy, and pot and kettle, black, black. (1943)

Source: Glenway Wescott. *Continual Lessons: The Journals of Glenway Wescott, 1937–1955* (ed. by Robert Phelps and Jerry Rosco). NY: Farrar, Straus & Giroux, 1990.

480. **Mae West** (1892–1980), Brooklyn-born film actress

The Brooklyn I was born in . . . was still a city of churches, with their great bronze bells walloping to the faithful from early dawn, and a city of waterfront dives where the old forest of the spars of sailing ships was rapidly being replaced by funnels and the Sands Street Navy Yard already had a reputation of girl chasers. Gentlemen, and deer, ran wild in Prospect Park. I was born in a world of much more sunlight and less smoke than now, a world of ringing horse cars, ragtime music, cakewalks, and Floradora sextets. . . . (1975)

Note: West describes Brooklyn of the 1890s.
Source: Ralph Monti. *I Remember Brooklyn: Memoirs from Famous Sons and Daughters.* NY: Carol Publishing, 1991.

481. **Wayne W. Westbrook** (1939–), American author and literary critic

Wall Street fired the minds and passions! It had helped turn America into an industrial and manufacturing beehive! It had spawned millionaires! It had shaped an aristocracy out of the plutocracy! . . . Wall Street traces a volatile path through American history, a repetitive cycle of ups and downs of business activity. The fact that the stock market had gone through such boom and bust periods fired many minds and passions into believing a good story is there. (1980)

> *Note: Westbrook refers to Wall Street as a subject of inspiration for fiction writers.*
> Source: Wayne W. Westbrook. *Wall Street in the American Novel.* NY: New York University Press, 1980.

482. **Richard J. Whalen** (1935–), American author

The truly terrible costs of New York are special and spiritual. These accruc in endless human discomfort, inconvenience, harassment and fear which have become a part of the pervasive background, like the noise and the filth, but are much deadlier. . . . If people are driven and their senses dulled, if they are alienated and dehumanized, the city is on the way to destroying itself. (1965)

> Source: Richard Whalen. *A City Destroying Itself: An Angry View of New York.* NY: Morrow, 1965.

483. **Edith Wharton** (1862–1937), American author, poet, and literary critic

Boston always *has* been self-conscious about Boston, but the one distinction of ugly, patchy, scrappy New York was that it didn't get off from itself and measure and generalise; it had that in common with Paris and London, but now it hasn't any longer. (1913)

Source: R. W. B. Lewis. *Edith Wharton: A Biography.* NY: Harper & Row, 1975.

◆ ◆ ◆

New York tolerated hypocrisy in private relations, but in business matters it expected a limpid and impeccable honesty. (1920)

Source: Edith Wharton. *The Age of Innocence.* NY: C. Scribner's Sons, 1968 (reprint of 1920 ed.).

484. **Charles Whibley** (1859–1930), English essayist and literary critic

As America is less a country than a collection of countries so New York is not a city—it is a collection of cities. . . . [H]ere . . . is room for men and women of every face and every race . . . all nationalities meet with an equal and a flattering acceptance. (1907)

Source: Charles Whibley. *American Sketches.* London/Edinburgh: Blackwood & Sons, 1908.

485. **Edmund White** (1940–), American novelist and short story writer

In the post-Stonewall decade there is a new quality to New York gay life. We don't hate ourselves so much (although I do wish everyone would stop picking on drag queens; I at least continue to see them as the saints of Bleecker Street). In general, we're kinder to our friends. Discovering that a celebrity is gay does not automatically lower him now in our eyes. . . . [T]he self-acceptance of the seventies might just give us the courage to experiment with new forms of love and camaraderie, including the marriage-blanc, the three-or-four way marriage bi or threesexuality. . . . (1991)

Note: White describes gay life of NYC in the 1970s.
Source: *The Faber Book of Gay Short Stories.* London/Boston: Faber & Faber, 1991.

486. **E. B. (Elwin Brooks) White** (1899–1985), American author, journalist, and editor

New York is to the nation what the white spire is to the village—the visible symbol of aspiration and faith, the white plume saying the way is up! (1962)

Source: *Mental Health in the Metropolis: The Mid-town Manhattan Study.* NY: Blackston Division/McGraw-Hill, 1962.

◆ ◆ ◆

A poem compresses much in a small space and adds music, thus heightening its meaning. The city [NYC] is like poetry: it compresses all life, all races and breeds into a small island and adds music and the accompaniment of internal engines. (1977)

Source: E. B. White. *Essays of E. B. White.* NY: Harper & Row, 1977.

◆ ◆ ◆

New York is part of the natural world. I love the city. I love the country . . . the city is part of the country. When I had an apartment on East Forty-Eighth Street, my backyard during the migratory season yielded more birds than I ever saw in Maine. . . . (1985)

Source: George Plimpton, ed. *Writers at Work: The Paris Review Interviews.* NY: Penguin Books, 1988 (8th series).

487. **Walt Whitman** (1819–1892), American poet, journalist, and author

Manhatta (poem)

. . .

The countless masts, the white shore steamers,
the lighters, the ferry boats, the black sea-steamers well
model'd,
The down-town streets, the jobbers' houses of business, the
houses of business of the ship-merchants and money-
brokers, the river streets,
Immigrants arriving, fifteen or twenty thousand in a week.
. . . (1855)

♦ ♦ ♦

Manhattan (poem)

. . .

The beautiful city, the city of hurried and sparkling
waters! the city of spires and masts!
The city nested in bays! my city!
The city of such women, I am mad with them! I will
return after death to be with them!
The city of such young men, I swear I cannot live
happy without I often go talk, walk, eat, drink,
sleep with them! (1860)

♦ ♦ ♦

More and more too, the *old name* absorbs into me-
MANNAHATTA, the "place encircled by many swift tides
and sparkling waters". How fit a name for America's great
democratic island city! The word itself, how beautiful! how
aboriginal! how it seems to rise with tall spires, glistening in
sunshine, with such New World atmosphere, vista and action! (1879)

Source: Walt Whitman. *The Complete Poetry and Prose of Walt
Whitman.* NY: Pellegrini & Cudahi, 1948.

488. **Elie Wiesel** (1928–), American author, Nobel Prize winner for literature, 1986

I have lived here [NYC] for some twenty years, more than anywhere in the world, and yet I have devoted only a few pages to New York in *The Accident* and one chapter in the *Gates of the Forest*. Why? Because I have not yet exhausted my childhood. Words grow, age, die, and I am still interested in that metamorphosis. And the words I use are still those that relate to my childhood. (1978)

Source: George Plimpton, ed. *Writers at Work: The Paris Review Interviews.* NY: Penguin Books, 1988 (8th series).

489. **Oscar Wilde** (1854–1900), English (Irish-born) playwright

Though one can dine in New York [NYC], one could not dwell there. (1887)

Source: *Court & Society Review* (British publication). March 1887.

490. **Elliot Willensky** (1933–), Brooklyn-born historian of Brooklyn

[W]hen vacant lots could still be found in Brooklyn, the warm weather months couldn't go by without the appearance of at least one carnival, block party . . . they weren't very impressive in the daytime, but once the sun set, the lights and motion and smells and rides made them mini-Coney Islands. Sponsorship as part of the local parish bazaar made gambling okay, and so the other sounds of the night were joined by the incessant *ticky-ticky-ticky* of spins of the wheels of chance. (1986)

◆ ◆ ◆

They (Brooklynites) were so easy to identify. You had only to listen to the way most of them spoke English. It was really no surprise that so many used the distinctive vernacular

branded "Brooklynese", even though its jarring mispro-
nunciations, ostentatious dentalizations, and curious inflec-
tions were by no means limited only to Brooklyn. The parents and grandparents of most of those with provincial
pronunciation were often first-generation Americans, many
not long off the boat. (1986)

Note: Willensky describes Brooklyn during 1920–1950s.
Source: Elliot Willensky. *When Brooklyn Was the World, 1920–
1957.* NY: Harmony Books, 1986.

491. **Tennessee Williams** (1911–1983), American dramatist

I particularly like New York [NYC] on hot summer nights
when all the . . . uh, superflous people are off the streets.
(1977)

Source: Gore Vidal. *Matters of Fact and Fiction: Essays,
1973–1976.* NY: Random House, 1977.

492. **Edmund Wilson** (1895–1972), American author, playwright, and literary critic

From the moment a New Yorker is confronted with almost
any large city of Europe, it is impossible for him to pretend
to himself that his own city is anything other than an un-
scrupulous real-estate speculation. (1947)

Source: Edmund Wilson. *Europe without Baedeker: Sketches
among the Ruins of Italy, Greece and England.* NY: Doubleday,
1947.

◆ ◆ ◆

In Brooklyn, in the neighborhood of Henry Street, the pleasant red and pink brick houses still worthily represent the
generation of Henry Ward Beecher, but an eternal Sunday is
on them now; they seem sunk in a final silence. (1925)

Source: Edmund Wilson. *A Literary Chronicle, 1920–1950*. Gloucester, MA: P. Smith, 1962 (reprint of 1956 ed.).

493. **Harry L. Wilson** (1867–1939), American author

A little strip of an island [Manhattan] with a row of well-fed folks up and down the middle, and a lot of hungry folks on each side. (1902)

Source: Harry L. Wilson. *The Spenders: A Tale of the Third Generation*. NY: Grosset & Dunlap, 1902.

494. **Walter Winchell** (1897–1972), American author and journalist

[Broadway] . . . where people spend money they haven't earned to buy things they don't need to impress people they don't like. (c. 1960)

Source: Eugene Brussells, ed. *Webster's New World Dictionary of Quotable Definitions*. 2d ed. Englewood Cliffs, NJ: Prentice Hall, 1988.

495. **P. G. (Pelham Grenville) Wodehouse** (1881–1975), American English-born author, essayist, and editor

The Sheridan Apartment House stands in the heart of New York's Bohemian and artistic quarter. If you threw a brick from any of its windows you could be certain to brain some rising interior decorator, some Vorticist sculptor or a writer of revolutionary Vers Libre. (1927)

Source: P. G. Wodehouse. *The Small Bachelor*. NY: George Doran, 1927.

496. **Thomas Wolfe** (1900–1938), American novelist

Proud, cruel, everchanging and ephemeral city [NYC], to

whom we came once when our hearts were high, our blood passionate and hot, our brain a particle of fire infinite and mutable city, mercurial city, strange citadel of million visaged time! Oh! endless river and eternal rock, in which the forms of life came, passed and changed intolerably before us, and to which we came, as every youth has come, with such enormous madness, and with so mad a hope—for what? . . . (1935)

Source: Thomas Wolfe. *Of Time and the River: A Legend of Man's Hunger in His Youth.* NY: C. Scribner's Sons, 1935.

◆ ◆ ◆

It [NYC] was a cruel city, but it was a lovely one, a savage city, yet it had such tenderness, a bitter, harsh and violent catacomb of stone and steel and tunneled rock, slashed savagely with light, and roaring, fighting a constant ceaseless warfare of men and machinery; and yet it was so sweetly and so delicately pulsed, as full of warmth, of passion, and of love, as it was full of hate. (1937)

Source: Thomas Wolfe. *The Web and the Rock.* NY: Harper & Row, 1986 (reprint of 1937 ed.).

◆ ◆ ◆

That was a good time then, for then the sun came out one day and the bridge [Brooklyn Bridge] made music through the shining air. It was like a song: it soared like flight above the harbor. . . . And I saw all the faces of the people on the bridge, and they were coming towards me and there was something strange and sad about it, and yet it was the most magnificent thing I had ever seen: the air was clean and sparkling like sapphires, and out beyond this was the harbor and I knew that the sea was there. (1937)

Source: Thomas Wolfe. *The Web and the Rock.* NY: Harper & Row, 1986 (reprint of 1937 ed.).

497. **Tom Wolfe** (1931–   ), American novelist

You know, it's funny on Saturday in New York, especially on
one of those Indian Summer days—God, somehow Culture just
seems to be in the air, like part of the weather, all the antique
shops on Madison Avenue, with a little blaze of golden ormolu
here, and a little oxblood-red leathery marquetry there, and the
rugs hung up in the second-floor display windows—rich!—a
Bakhtiari with a little pale yellow setting off the red—and the
galleries. God, gallery after gallery, with the pristine white walls
of Culture, the black wooden floors, and the Culture buds, a little Renoirish softness in the autumn faces. (1968)

Source: Tom Wolfe. *The Pump House Gang.* NY: Farrar, Straus
& Giroux, 1968.

◆ ◆ ◆

Oh, to be young and come to New York and move into your
first loft and look at the world with eyes that lit up even the
rotting fire-escape railings, even the buckling pressed tin
squares on the ceiling, even the street-metal shower stall
with belly dents and rusting seams . . . the door with its crow-
bar history of twenty five years of break-ins . . . the in-
domitable roach that appears in every morning in silhouette
on the cord of the hot plate . . . the two cats nobody ever
housebroke . . . the bag ladies who sit on the standpipes
swabbing the lesions on their ankles. . . . (1987)

Source: Tom Wolfe. *Bonfire of the Vanities.* NY: Farrar, Straus &
Giroux, 1987.

498. **Alfred Wood** (1826–1895), American Civil War colonel,
real estate speculator in Queens Borough

Real Estate Prospectus (poem)
Who are fond of charming music
    and rural lunches besides,

And would love to make some money
and enjoy a jolly ride,
Ye mechanics, bankers, merchants,
pretty maids and gallants gay
Come with us to Inglewood for
a glorious gala day! (1872)

Note: Colonel Wood provided transportation, free food, and music to sell real estate.
Source: Vincent F. Seyfried. *The Story of Queens Village.* NY: Queens Village Centennial Association, 1974.

499. **Cornel Woolrich** (1903–1968), American crime/suspense novelist

No place like it [NYC] for living. And probably no place like it for dying. (1970)

Source: *Ellery Queen's Mystery Magazine.* December 1970.

500. **Lady Emmeline Stuart Wortley** (1806–1855), English author and poet

The views from the heights of the cemetery [Greenwood Cemetery, Brooklyn] were sublime. I admired the one from Ocean Hill the most. There is a lovely variety of valleys, elevations, plains, groves, and glades, and paths. When will London have anything even approaching to this magnificent *cemetery?* The ocean rolling and moaning, with its fine melancholy, organ-like sounds, so near, like a mighty mourner, she cannot have. (1849)

Source: Lady Emmeline Wortley. *Travels in the United States During 1849 and 1850.* NY: Harper & Brothers, 1851.

501. **Frank Lloyd Wright** (1869–1959), American architect and author

New York is the biggest mouth in the world. It appears to be an example of herd instinct, leading the universal urban conspiracy to beguile man from his birthright (the good ground), to hang him by his eye-brows from skyhooks above hard pavement, to crucify him, sell him, or be sold by him. (1954)

Source: Frank Lloyd Wright. *The Living City.* NY: Horizon Press, 1954.

502. **Malcolm X** (1920–1962), African American militant leader; born Malcolm Little, changed name to El-Hajj Malik El Shabazz

Up and down along and between Lenox and Seventh and Eighth Avenues, Harlem was like some technicolor bazaar. Hundreds of Negro soldiers and sailors, gawking and young like me, passed by. . . . [T]here had already been some muggings and robberies. . . . Blacktown crawled with white people, with pimps, prostitutes, bootleggers, with hustlers of all kind, with colorful characters, and with police and prohibition agents. (1964)

♦ ♦ ♦

Every layover night in Harlem, I ran and explored new places. . . . I combed not only bright-light areas, but Harlem's residential areas from best to worst . . . dirt, garbage cans overflowing or kicked over, drunks, dope addicts, beggars, sleazy bars, store front churches . . . "bargain" stores, hock-shops, undertaking parlors, greasy "home-cooking" restaurants, beauty shops. . . . But New York was heaven to me. And Harlem was seventh heaven. (1964)

Note: In both of these passages, Malcolm X refers to Harlem of the 1940s.
Source: Malcolm X. *The Autobiography of Malcolm X.* NY: Ballantine Books, 1964.

503. **E. Idell Zeisloft** (NDA), American author and editor

On the Island of Manhattan the people may be divided into seven classes: the very rich, the rich, the prosperous, the well-to-do comfortable, the well-to-do uncomfortable, the comfortable or contented poor, and the submerged or uncomfortable poor. (1899)

Source: E. Idell Zeisloft, ed. *The New Metropolis: 1600-Memorable Events of Three Centuries-1900, New York.* NY: D. Appleton & Co., 1899.

Subject Index

Note: Numbers are entry numbers, not page numbers.

Chronological Index

About the Author

VLADIMIR F. WERTSMAN graduated from University A. I. Cuza Law School (Romania) and earned his master's degree in library science from Columbia University (1967). He served as Adult Services Librarian and Branch Librarian in various branches of the Brooklyn Public Library, was Russian and Romanian languages specialist at Donnell Foreign Language Library, New York, and worked as Senior Librarian at the Job Information Center, Mid-Manhattan Library, New York. He is a member of the American Romanian Academy of Arts and Sciences, International Social Science Honor Society, American Association for the Advancement of Slavic Studies, and the American Library Association. He chaired the PLA/Multilingual Library Service Committee and presently is Chair of Publishers and Multicultural Materials Committee of Ethnic Materials Round Table, American Library Association. He is the author of *The Romanians in America, 1748–1974* (Oceana, 1975), *The Ukrainians in America, 1608–1975* (Oceana, 1976), *The Russians in America, 1727–1976* (Oceana, 1977), *The Armenians in America, 1616–1976* (Oceana, 1978), *The Romanians in America and Canada* (Gale Research, 1980), *The Librarian's Companion* (Greenwood Press, 1987), *Career Opportunities for Bilinguals and Multilinguals,* second edition (Scarecrow Press, 1994), *Directory of Ethnic and Multicultural Publishers, Distributors, and Resource Organizations,* third edition (Ethnic Materials Information Exchange Round Table, ALA, 1995), and *What's Cooking in Multicultural America: An Annotated Bibliographic Guide to over Four Hundred Ethnic Cuisines* (Scarecrow Press, 1996); and co-author of *Ukrainians in Canada and the United States* (Gale Research, 1981) and *Free Voices in Russian Literature, 1950s–1980s* (Russica, 1987). His biography is included in *Who's Who in America* (47th–50th eds.) and *Contemporary Authors* (New Revision Series).